Equality
Is Not Enough

Seeking Full Liberty
For Lesbian, Gay, Bisexual, and
Transgender People

Andrew S. Park

Callowhill Publishing
New York, NY

Equality Is Not Enough/ Andrew S. Park. —1st ed.
ISBN 978-0-9896829-0-9

Contents

Introduction

This book outlines how the lesbian, gay, bisexual, and transgender (LGBT) movement can establish an agenda based on the lived experiences of LGBT people, who want not only equality, but freedom, dignity, and well-being. LGBT people seek fulfillment in all aspects of their lives, not just those moments where their LGBT identities are the most prominent. Improving the lives of people begins with understanding their current lived experiences; and it continues with knowing what programs can improve those lives in ways that are meaningful and positive. I propose that the LGBT movement in the United States adopt frameworks developed in other parts of the world, the goals of which are to enhance people's freedoms to live the lives of their choosing.

In Chapter 1, I look at some of the benchmarks of the LGBT equality movement from my own personal perspective as an advocate for LGBT people. I have spent nearly thirty years working for equal rights, initially as a trial attorney and Administrative Judge for the US Equal Employment Opportunity Commission, then as a local activist in legal communities, for the Democratic Party, and in political races. I founded and directed a legal advocacy organization for LGBT people, and I have travelled to some of the world's hotspots of LGBT activism. Though I have seen tremendous advancements for LGBT equality, I have also seen how laws can fall short of their purposes. I highlight some of the gaps between the agenda for LGBT equality and the lived experiences of LGBT people, some of whom have been my clients, my friends, and fellow members of the LGBT community. The LGBT movement must continue every effort to achieve legal equality, and I believe that it will be successful. But equality is not enough. We need to identify how millions of LGBT people can achieve better lives.

Many people have proposed frameworks for improving the lives of LGBT people. In Chapter 2, I review some of the perspectives that have had significant support during the last century. For many decades, professionals and advocates sought to treat homosexuality and gender deviance as a disease, forcing psychological and physical cures and conversions. At other points in American culture, the spotlight was placed on groups—the homophobic majority and the oppressed minority. At other points, the target became governments and other powerful institutions. Advocacy goals centered on reforming these institutions so that they would treat LGBT people the same as non-LGBT people. These increasingly empowered views of sexual orientation and gender identity have resulted in important advances for LGBT people as a collective group, but the focus must shift to LGBT people as individuals.

In Chapters 3 and 4, I develop a framework that the LGBT movement can use to formulate its priorities for achieving better lives for LGBT people. The first step is to understand the current lived experiences of LGBT people. In Chapter 3, I discuss how prejudice and stigma fence in LGBT people and how the demand to convert, pretend, and cover can cause LGBT people to limit their own behavior and capabilities in ways that are as powerful as legal inequality. Concern with the lived experiences of LGBT people should be based on evidence about the development of LGBT people. I review some frameworks for personality and identity development for sexual orientation and gender identity and the need for more work in this area.

Building on what we know about the lived experiences of LGBT people, I propose in Chapter 4 a framework for setting a movement-wide agenda. I look to the field of human development and suggest that we adopt the *capabilities approach* currently being used by development agencies in all parts of the world (and, indeed, by many LGBT groups in the United States). The goal of the approach is to increase each person's freedoms and opportunities to live a better life of their choice. I identify specific capabilities that each person must have in order to preserve dignity and well-being. These include bodily health, intellectual and emotional capacity, housing, work, chosen family, culture, and control over governance.

This conception of a better life provides a foundation for a post-equality LGBT movement. In Chapter 5, I explain why the capabilities approach would help the LGBT movement build on recent advancements. The approach helps activists look at the gap between the legal standards they have achieved and the continuing need to implement and enforce those standards. It prioritizes rights that are at the core of the LGBT movement, such as choice, autonomy, and consent. It also incorporates a list of human rights that have already been identified by LGBT communities in America and other parts of the world. Most importantly, the capabilities approach recognizes the diversity of identities. Rather than endorsing a particular LGBT identity, it seeks to increase capabilities of individuals to choose their own identities. If the capabilities of an LGBT person are limited by racial, gender, or economic dynamics then the approach requires a direct response to these differences. Without attending to issues such as race, gender and economics, where such issues are relevant, the approach cannot be successful. The approach accounts for the multiple factors that can hold each LGBT person back from the life of his or her choosing.

Chapter 6 sets out steps to implement the capabilities approach. I look at the familiar areas of LGBT advocacy such as employment, identity documentation, and school safety to illustrate how the movement would expand from equality advocacy to the capabilities approach. Gathering data would become a central part of such an agenda, as would a shift to programs focused on specific populations. Demographic information about the LGBT movement has already become a core part of LGBT advocacy. In areas such as school safety and support for seniors the LGBT movement is already mounting effective efforts to gather data and construct programs to focus on the well-being of individuals. I suggest how these can be expanded to address the well-being of LGBT people in a greater number of areas.

I also propose the creation of an American LGBT wellness index. This index would measure a variety of aspects of well-being in the LGBT population. While it might include one composite score that could be used for purposes of media communication and policy making, the underlying data would disaggregate how different subcomponents of the community are faring in a number of categories.

In the concluding chapter, I argue that the end game of this approach is to embrace the goodness of each LGBT person. The capabilities approach provides an opportunity for the LGBT movement to pierce the moral bracket that it often uses when advocating for equality.

The movement should claim not only legal equality, but moral equality as well.

The concepts I introduce apply to lesbian, gay, and bisexual people as well as transgender people. In many instances I refer to research on sexual orientation separately from research on gender identity. Conclusions about sexual orientation are not automatically transferable to gender identity and expression, and vice versa. Furthermore, the volume of research and data about lesbian and gay people is greater than what is available for transgender people. The relative differences in data do not detract from my collective conclusions and recommendations. Gaps in knowledge only prescribe different tasks to make sure our information is complete. Each person has a sexual orientation and a gender identity. The right to a path towards a better life is common to all, regardless of sexual orientation and gender identity.

- 1 -

The Promise of Liberty

On June 26, 2015, the US Supreme Court issued an historic decision recognizing marriage equality for same-sex couples. This decision was the result of decades of advocacy by LGBT people and their allies. Writing on behalf of the Court, Justice Kennedy traced the progress of LGBT rights. He recalled that just over a decade earlier, the Court had struck down laws "that made same-sex intimacy a criminal act."[1] But, he noted, even though the Court's earlier decisions allowed "individuals to engage in intimate association without criminal liability, it does not follow that freedom stops there. Outlaw to outcast may be a step forward, but it does not achieve the full promise of liberty."[2]

What is the 'full promise of liberty' to which Justice Kennedy refers? In the summer of 2015, the promise of liberty meant the recognition of the equal right to marry for same-sex couples. As debates about the rights of LGBT people progress through more advanced stages, that promise will take the shape of the many struggles and injustices that LGBT people continue to face. Ultimately, liberty goes beyond what the law can provide. In this book I propose that the promise of liberty will ultimately be revealed by the capability of each person to live a life of their choosing.

As a society, the question of how to define full liberty for LGBT people is a relatively recent one. Looking back a decade earlier, the current successes did not seem within reach. In 2004, so-called "defense of marriage" amendments were adopted throughout the country, part of a demoralizing losing streak of over thirty ballot initiatives that enshrined discrimination into state constitutions and legal systems. George W. Bush, a vocal opponent of LGBT equality, was re-elected president. Many analysts advanced the narrative that the right wing had used marriage as a wedge issue to turn out its base of 'value voters.' This narrative helped cement the notion that LGBT people fell outside of American values.

In 2008, the voters of California approved Proposition 8, amending the state's constitution to prohibit same-sex marriage. The nation elected a president who had not yet embraced marriage equality.

Initially, advocates sought equality through a campaign that focused on the benefits and responsibilities that came with marriage. After several defeats and a great deal of resources to analyze why those defeats happened, advocates began efforts to put the concepts of love and commitment at the center of the public messages. In the courts, litigants continued to focus on state marriage bans in an attempt to create a patchwork of marriage equality jurisdictions. A visible shift could be seen by the end of 2010. President Barack Obama, who had previously opposed same-sex marriage, said that his views were evolving. Congress repealed the "Don't Ask, Don't Tell" policy in December of that year. Over the next thirty months, state legislatures began taking up the issue and voters in three states approved same-sex marriage.

On June 26, 2013, the LGBT community won big at the national level. The US Supreme Court said that the federal government must recognize same-sex marriages where they were validly entered into at the state level. Section three of the Defense of Marriage Act had prevented tens of thousands of married couples from accessing federal rights as married people. The Court said that the provision "is invalid, for no legitimate purpose overcomes the purpose and effect to disparage and to injure those whom the State, by its marriage laws, sought to protect in personhood and dignity."[3]

Litigation by same-sex couples erupted in state and federal courts in all parts of the country. By 2015, the

LGBT community succeeded in successfully framing marriage equality as an issue of basic equality and civil rights.[4] The decision that summer, recognizing the constitutional right to marriage equality, was historic, but it was by no means an unexpected leap forward. No single event or act triggered a "tipping point." Rather, the change occurred the way social change often does. At some point support for the issue went from less than fifty percent to slightly more than fifty percent.

Advocacy in the US Supreme Court followed decades of litigation and public education. Due to the work of determined advocates, public support had been creeping up year after year. In each of the previous marriage battles the gay community had been learning to craft effective messages, create alliances with other groups, talk to voters one at a time, and build organizations, donor bases, databases, and volunteer forces. Although the "values voter" debates of 2004 seem distant now, that distance has been created by LGBT advocates who have plugged away at the same battle for years.

The Equality Agenda

Support for LGBT equality has continued to increase even during those times when courts and electorates rejected pro-LGBT policies. Constitutional scholar Jules Lobel calls this evolution of the legal standards "success without victory."[5] No one knows this dynamic better than Evan Wolfson. As an attorney for Lambda Legal Defense and Education Fund (also referred to as just Lambda), he represented James Dale against the Boy Scouts of America when Dale was expelled in 1990 from his position as an assistant scoutmaster because he was gay. In 2000, the Supreme Court ruled in favor of the Boy Scouts, concluding that their constitutional rights to freedom of association protected their ability to exclude homosexuals.[6] By the result of the lawsuit, the case was a defeat for LGBT equality. However, looking at the movement and the country, the case was an enormous success. Wolfson and his client ignited a national debate. Boy Scout troops meet in public buildings, church basements, and public parks in every community in America, and the debate touched communities across the country. Conversations about the visibility of gay men, the validity of stereotypes, and the role of government played out in city councils, in the philanthropic sector, in churches, on the covers of news magazines, and within families.

The message of LGBT advocates was one firmly grounded in the equal opportunity paradigm of the African-American civil rights movement: James Dale should have been judged on his merits. His identity as a gay man should not render him unfit for leadership in the organization.

Wolfson eventually left Lambda and formed Freedom to Marry, the organization that has spearheaded the movement for marriage equality. There he advocated similar messages. The first was a singular claim that the opportunity to marry is an issue of equal inclusion in society. Strategically, Wolfson sought to "lose forward"—the campaigning process for each loss would leave in its wake incremental increases in support, greater knowledge about how to wage the battle, and a stronger community infrastructure.

Though marriage has become the most visible LGBT issue, it is only one of many goals that are important to LGBT people. To me, the issue of marriage equality is a good example of how shifting priorities in the LGBT community develop and resolve. I first encountered the issue of marriage equality in a formal way in the late 1980s when I helped organize a public debate in Washington, DC, on the topic of whether marriage should be a priority for the LGBT community. Tom Stoddard and Paula Ettlebrick, two lawyers from Lambda, engaged in what struck me as a sincere, well-reasoned model of airing different points of view within the community. Stoddard and Ettlebrick choreographed a debate in which Stoddard presented the view that full lesbian and gay equality meant seeking "gay marriage" (that is what we called it), while Ettlebrick represented the view that marriage has not been a helpful institution for others seeking equality, particularly women and girls. She raised the questions of whether seeking marriage as a path to equality would strengthen social preferences for married people and disapproval of single people. They took the debate on the road and gave groups around the country a smart way to hear the arguments and engage in the debate.

At that time, the marriage debate seemed out of reach for lesbian and gay activists in most states. Though viable advocacy was developing in Vermont and Hawaii, the rest of the country was not near the point of considering specific policy changes. Rather, LGBT activists concerned with the legal recognition of couples were seeking recognition through expanded definitions of household or the adoption of domestic partnership ordinances. Some activists saw this as a way to broaden the types of family relationships receiving recognition and shift the traditional attachment to marriage as the only institution to legitimize relationships. At the same time, the women's movement was advocating for workplace, family, and medical leave policies at the state and federal level. These policies defined family in ways that reflected updated economic realities of workers. Meanwhile, conservatives were advocating marriage promotion within welfare reform.

In 1990, I had just become the first co-chair of the Gay and Lesbian Attorneys of Washington, DC (GAYLAW), the group that hosted the Stoddard and Ettlebrick debate. We were in the midst of lobbying the DC City Council for passage of a local domestic partnership ordinance called the Healthcare Benefits Expansion Act. My then-partner and I were the fourth couple to register when the act was finally adopted. Personally, I have been a supporter of the view espoused by Ettlebrick. It still does not make much sense to me that marriage should be a factor in deciding how you can be sued for hitting someone with a car, how many pine trees on your family farm are covered by a state tax benefit, or whether a child in the household has to pay thousands of dollars for braces. Nevertheless, like Ettlebrick, I supported the notion that we should all have the legal opportunity to be married.

My support for marriage equality grew a few years later, however, when I had the occasion to quantitatively examine how the inability to marry affected people. Like others, I had seen the studies concluding that 1,138 rights at the federal level were tied to marriage.[7] In Pennsylvania, we conducted our own study, which identified nearly 700 additional rights in state law that were tied to marriage.[8] These ranged from hospital visitation rights to the ability to deduct farming expenses from ones tax return to exemptions from real estate transfer taxes. The number of rights does not represent real couples. Most of the provisions of these laws are particular to a set of circumstances that only some couples will experience. Counting rights in this way was more about counting government decisions than counting the lived experiences of real people. I wanted to know how the inability to get married affected members of the community using data gathered from those people. One crude, though easily available set of data was the tracking numbers kept by legal organizations that received calls from LGBT individuals.

I spoke to the people who managed the phone intake lines at the national and regional offices of Lambda, the National Center for Lesbian Rights (NCLR), the national and state chapters of the American Civil Liberties Union (ACLU), the Gay and Lesbian Advocates and Defenders (GLAD), and several community centers that operated legal counseling services, youth centers, and anti-violence projects. I asked them to categorize the calls they received according to the issues that were being raised by the callers. All of the groups received calls on a wide variety of issues.

What surprised me was the consistency of how the issues were distributed. Issues of custody and parenting were the largest proportion of calls, followed by issues of relationship formation or dissolution between same-sex couples. Other issues varied in the proportion of calls, but four other issues seem to always be present. Employment discrimination was an issue faced by callers to all groups but was particularly experienced by trans workers. At least as common were issues of immigration and asylum. School based harassment, particularly from gender variant students, was also prevalent, as were reports of neighbor-to-neighbor harassment.

To me, this represented rough yet meaningful evidence of the lived experiences of LGBT people. Over half of all the calls related to parenting and couples problems, and many of those calls were related to the lack of a framework to resolve the disputes. For most of the callers, a single policy would have solved the issue underlying these calls: equal marriage rights. The Employment Non-Discrimination Act (ENDA), immigration reform, federal hate crimes law—none of those would have helped as many people as marriage rights. Could a system of alternative relationships be better? I think so; and I envy the ability of activists in Europe and Latin America who are able to more easily engage in discussions around sensible, tailored forms of family recognition. Advocates will continue to craft policies that make sense in the specific context of each issue. Public policy will continue to evolve to recognize families. Nevertheless, the fact that marriage offers a potential immediate solution to the problems of so many people means that we must recognize its importance as a legitimate policy goal.

Ultimately, marriage equality has captured the energy of more people than any other movement goal. Many gay men and lesbians see marriage as a priority, allies understand the goal, and it is a symbolic rallying point that has received more grassroots support in recent years than most other LGBT issues combined. People do not petition door to door in order to pass an employment non-discrimination act. Safe schools advocacy does not attract tens of thousands of people making small donations to LGBT groups. Marriage has become a priority because a critical number of Americans see it as one.

In November 2008, after California passed Proposition 8, which amended the constitution to stop same-sex couples from continuing to marry, a series of rallies were held across the country to protest the adoption of the amendment, as well as question the role of the Mormon Church in funding the campaign in favor of the amendment. In New York City, a rally organized in just a few days became the biggest LGBT protest that the city had seen in several years, growing to such unexpected size that police had to shut down traffic around the lower part of Central Park simply to accommodate the crowds.

I attended the rally with Matt Foreman, former Executive Director of the National Gay and Lesbian Task Force (NGLTF), who has attended far more rallies then me. There, we saw lots of signs, lots of youth, lots of straight people, and lots of men and women. We both were struck by what we did not see: indications that the leading LGBT groups had orchestrated this rally. There were no logos, no glossy literature, no speakers except for those who showed up with their own bullhorns and portable sound systems, and not much of a pre-event press strategy. In fact, CNN did not cover the event until the crowd expanded to Columbus Circle and shut down traffic in front of the CNN offices. Following the event, the media coverage was strong, and local activists were effective in raising questions about the Mormon Church's support of anti-gay efforts. I doubt, however, that even they expected that large of a crowd.

The marriage argument has been successful, in part, because LGBT leaders have reshaped the discussion from one of special rights to one of equality. As Evan Wolfson has said so many times, it is not "gay marriage," it is simply "marriage." He points to the importance of marriage in American culture and concludes that lesbian and gay Americans are treated unequally because they are excluded from it. After evolving beyond the emphasis on privacy, which had been the primary argument used by the LGBT community to combat laws criminalizing same-sex sexual conduct, equality is now the centerpiece of arguments for gay rights. Unequal treatment by any institution is challenged, regardless of whether that institution is the US Army, a religious seminary, a country club, or a welfare program.

The Equality Organizations

As we look at the largest organizational voices in the LGBT community, equality has become the central focus of the movement. The Human Rights Campaign (HRC) is the largest gay advocacy group, with headquarters in Washington, DC, a combined budget of $50 million in political and charitable funding, and the movement's most robust fundraising and communications operation. The logo, a yellow equal sign on a blue background, is the bumper sticker logo of the LGBT community. HRC's mission revolves around the priority of equality:

> By inspiring and engaging all Americans, HRC strives to end discrimination against LGBT citizens and realize a nation that achieves fundamental fairness and equality for all.
>
> HRC seeks to improve the lives of LGBT Americans by advocating for equal rights and benefits in the workplace, ensuring families are treated equally under the law and increasing public support among all Americans through innovative advocacy, education and outreach programs. HRC works to secure equal rights for LGBT individuals and families at the federal and state levels by lobbying elected officials, mobilizing grassroots supporters, educating Americans, investing strategically to elect fair-minded officials and partnering with other LGBT organizations.[9]

The second largest organization, according to budget size, is the Lambda Legal Defense and Education Fund. Attorneys in its New York City headquarters and regional field offices litigate cases and conduct advocacy to change legal standards. The principle of equality is the central pillar of its mission:

> At Lambda Legal, we imagine a world without discrimination and inequality, and we work to achieve that vision every day. We make the case for equality in the nation's courts and in the court of public opinion…. We win legal victories for clients who seek equality on the job, protection for their parenting or relationship rights, equal access to health care, or protection against discrimination because of HIV status.[10]

The Gay and Lesbian Advocates and Defenders, located in Boston, MA, has led litigation in New England where marriage cases in Vermont, Massachusetts, and cases on the federal Defense of Marriage Act have been forward markers of LGBT legal progress. Its mission focuses on 'ending discrimination,' and both the National Center for Lesbian Rights and Lambda Legal's mission statements focus on 'civil rights.'

At the same time, groups at the state level have adopted the equality framework, as did the group that I founded, which eventually became Equality Pennsylvania. The largest state group, Equality California, says on its website, "Equality California works to achieve equality and secure legal protections for LGBT people." Equality Alabama, Equality Arizona, Georgia Equality, Equality Hawai'i, Equality Illinois, Indiana Equality, Equality Maine, Equality Maryland, Equality Michigan, Garden State Equality (New Jersey), Equality New Mexico, Equality North Carolina, Equality Ohio, Trans Ohio, the Equality Network (Oklahoma), Equality Pennsylvania, Marriage Equality Rhode Island, South Carolina Equality Coalition, Equality South Dakota, Tennessee Equality Project, Equality Texas, Equality Utah, Equality Virginia, and Equal Rights Washington are all state-level LGBT groups that embrace the equality agenda and use the word "equality" to communicate their mission. They, along with other groups, make up the Equality Federation, the network of state-based LGBT advocacy groups.

When Barack Obama put together his 2012 reelection campaign, the unifying principle was equality. He echoed this theme in his stump speech:

> You can choose to turn back the clock 50 years for women, and for immigrants, and for gays — or in this election, you can stand up for that basic principle that makes our country the envy of the world -- that we're all created equal; that everybody has a place. (Applause.) Black, white, Hispanic, Asian, Native American, young, old -- black, white -- (applause) -- gay, straight -- it doesn't matter, no matter who you are, no matter what you look like, no matter where you come from, no matter who you love — in America,

you've got to be able to make it if you try. (Applause.) That's what we believe. That's what we're fighting for. (Applause.)[11]

The consistent equality message has been successful. It is so pervasive that some might wonder if there is any other possible goal. Though it has been the focus of my life's work, legal equality is not enough.

Legal Equality is Not Enough

The LGBT movement must continue to work for full legal equality. This goal will require many more battles at all levels of government. However, good laws do not necessarily mean good lives. The approach of the current LGBT movement reflects, more or less, on the civil rights movements of the sixties and seventies. We know from these movements that legal equality does not provide a complete response to oppression. Employment nondiscrimination laws have not resulted in full workplace equality for women and African-Americans. The political system continues to be dominated by white men even though the right to vote and run for office was secured decades ago. Latino families face documented patterns of exclusion from housing, even where fair-housing laws exist. Patterns of differences along racial and ethnic lines persist even though fair school programs and affirmative action programs have been in place for years. As in any civil rights movement, formal legal equality will only be part of what each LGBT person needs to achieve the best life possible.

The shaky relationship between formal law and lived experience is a dynamic that the LGBT community has grappled with in both positive and negative ways. In 1986, the US Supreme Court upheld the right of states to criminalize homosexual sodomy. Facing a charge of sodomy brought against him by the state of Georgia, Michael

Hardwick claimed that the Georgia sodomy statute violated the US Constitution. The Supreme Court issued a highly criticized opinion citing a millennium of moral teaching, concluding that there was "no right to homosexual sodomy."[12] The day-to-day reality was that people were engaging in sodomy in all states. But the Court's opinion in this case was used by judges, policymakers, and anti-gay zealots alike to argue that LGBT people were unfit for full citizenship.

In early 1996, I founded the Center for Lesbian and Gay Civil Rights (the Center), an organization in Philadelphia, which provided legal services to LGBT people. The Center's initial board of directors included the leadership of many legal groups active in LGBT rights including the local chapter of the American Civil Liberties Union, the National Organization for Women, the public employee's union, and others. Starting weeks ahead we planned the public launch of the Center at a press conference on May 20, 1996, to be held at the Philadelphia Bar Association. We scheduled the conference in a way to ensure that television stations would send camera crews and put the event on the early evening news.

At 11:00 am on that same day, the US Supreme Court finally issued its historic decision striking down Colorado's Amendment 2.[13] The voters of Colorado had approved an amendment to Colorado's constitution that would have prevented any town or county in Colorado from adopting an anti-discrimination law protecting gay and lesbian people. Several localities in Colorado already had adopted such non-discrimination laws. The amendment invalidated those and prevented any local or state agency from taking future action to protect gay and lesbian people.

The Supreme Court struck down the law in what was the broadest legal victory the American lesbian and gay community had ever won. Justice Kennedy, who authored the opinion for the Supreme Court, said that the amendment basically removed essential rights of citizenship from lesbian and gay people. This, done on the basis of animus, was unconstitutional. The litigation had lasted for years, and the movement made hard strategic choices as the case moved from the Colorado court system to the US Supreme Court and then waited for an unusually long time for the Court to rule. It was a huge victory.

The opinion was short and focused on how the law potentially permitted state and local governments to strip lesbian and gay people of their ability to fully exercise their rights of citizenship. The Court did not address the fact that, according to earlier rulings of the same Supreme Court, it was still permissible to put lesbian and gay people in jail for having sex. The Supreme Court left lesbian and gay people in a bizarre legal status in which they were simultaneously citizens and outlaws. More than that, the sodomy laws left intact by the Supreme Court were used to support a variety of other anti-gay measures, including efforts to close a public library to gay groups, deny permanent residence to gay immigrants, prohibit gay men and lesbians from fostering or adopting children, prohibit gay and lesbian student groups on college campuses, oppose protection of gay people from discrimination in employment deny gay and lesbian Texans protection under the state hate crime laws, and deny public employment to gay people.[14]

Because of the unexpected overlap of the scheduling of our press conference and Supreme Court's ruling, what we had planned as an exciting but possibly wonky press conference turned out to be an announcement of an historic legal decision. It was a perfect coincidence. I found myself standing in the offices of the oldest bar association in the country (founded by Benjamin Franklin, no less), surrounded by progressive politicians and the legal elite with a microphone in my hand and a room of reporters who wanted to know what the decision meant. I celebrated the equality given to lesbian and gay people by the Court and insisted on the necessity to continue the battle to make this decision real for LGBT people in Pennsylvania. The local news channels and papers carried the story "Supreme Court issues gay rights decision, community forms legal group," as if the community had read the decision that morning, had a big lunch meeting, and formed the Center for Lesbian and Gay Civil Rights over dessert. It immediately put us on the Rolodex of the media establishment and propelled our efforts to enhance legal services for LGBT people in the region.

The truth, however, is that the vast majority of LGBT people we represented did not directly benefit from the Supreme Court's decision. With a staff of attorneys, law students, and social workers, we responded to hundreds of requests a year for help with custody, domestic violence, employment discrimination, health insurance coverage, gender classifications on government documents, school harassment, and other issues. The sweeping ruling of the Colorado case set a new direction in the echo-chamber of persuasion and supported litigation for some LGBT people, but it did not affect the daily needs of our clients.

For example, the decision did not affect the status of lesbians as parents in Pennsylvania. I focus here on lesbians because our caseload in this area was almost entirely women. At the Center, we received a large number of calls related to parenting issues. A year after our formation, we merged with a twenty-year-old organization called Custody Action for Lesbian Mothers (CALM) to form a project to represent lesbians and transgender mothers whose custody was being challenged based on their sexual orientation or gender identity. This issue reflects the lived experience of many lesbians, then and now. According to recent demographic data, nearly fifty percent of lesbians under 50 are raising children. Same-sex couples with children are more likely to be racial and ethnic minorities.[15]

In Pennsylvania, we had already won the equality argument in the area of custody for lesbians. The state's Supreme Court had held that homosexuality was not a proper basis for denying custody. However, our experience mirrored the experience of advocates across the country: the legal and social service system ignored its own rules. Family court judges continued to deny custody to lesbian and transgender mothers. Child welfare workers continued to apply standards to lesbian parents that were different than those applied to other parents. Lesbians and transgender women were told, after no inquiry whatsoever, that they would be a damaging influence on their children or that their children would become targets of stigma.

The fact that the law was on our side was evidenced by the fact that we rarely lost a case. However, we could only take a few cases at any given time. Our strategy was to fully take on the issue of sexual orientation and gender identity, bring in psychologists to provide child evaluations and expert testimony on the relevance of homosexuality, and argue the State's legal precedent. Few people could afford this kind of representation on their own, and those that could had a hard time finding it. When the Center started, not a single family law attorney advertised in any LGBT newspaper in the state. Local law schools did not offer classes on sexual orientation or gender identity. Judges received no training in LGBT family law. Most lesbian and transgender mothers fighting for custody in Pennsylvania did not benefit from the formal legal equality they were supposed to be getting.

Lesbians and transgender women (and later, men) seeking second parent adoption faced a perverse procedure. In order for a woman to adopt the child of her partner and become the second parent, her partner would have to give up parental rights. Only after the child was technically parentless could the couple then adopt the child together. Only one judge in the state was willing to grant second-parent adoptions. She held the hearings during lunch hour when her staff was out so that others in the same courthouse would not know what she was doing.

The general legal advice to lesbian couples in eastern Pennsylvania giving birth to a baby was "when you get ready to deliver, go to New Jersey and have the baby there." New Jersey courts, with far better provisions, would temporarily take jurisdiction over children born in New Jersey. With regard to the issue of parenting, the opportunity to have a parent-child relationship was not undermined by lack of equality as much as by lack of knowledge, lack of income, lack of access to the courts, lack of judicial competence, lack of community support, and geographic circumstance.

The Supreme Court's decision also did not address the virulent discrimination faced by transgender people. We regularly received calls about youth being harassed because of their gender expression, and in some cases those calls came from supportive and loving parents who wanted their children to be able to choose their own paths. In one such case, a young woman had gone through school using a name different than the one on her birth certificate. She wanted to have her chosen name on her high school diploma. The law (at least at that time) was on our side. Requests for name and gender changes should have been simple, but administrators and bureaucrats placed all sorts of roadblocks in our way.

The Colorado decision also did not change the fact that employers can legally harass and fire LGBT workers in Pennsylvania and, as of 2013, in 29 other states.[16] In my experience working as an Administrative Judge at the US Equal Employment Opportunity Commission, and then advocating on behalf of LGBT workers in Pennsylvania, different identities seem to face different patterns of discrimination in the workplace. Without understanding these patterns, we will not be able to craft appropriate equality laws with enforcement provisions. The data is very sparse, and our suppositions need to be tested.

The supposition that I have built over time is the following, stated in a very oversimplified and categorized way: Transgender workers, black lesbians, and black gay men face discrimination in the job application process at rates higher than others. White lesbians get hired, but are denied promotions at rates higher than others. White gay men are promoted but get harassed at rates higher than others. Of course, patterns of discrimination are complex and varied, and I cannot be sure whether the trends I perceived were real, but let us assume for a moment that they are. If these patterns are accurate, then achieving equality for transgender and African-American job applicants requires advocates to examine employers' hiring decisions. One method would be to compare data about the available pool of applicants to data about the workforce itself. For white lesbians, we would want a law that provides lost wages, but for white gay men we would want a law that compensates for harassment. Simply put, without more data, the LGBT community can not be certain that the Employment Nondiscrimination Act, currently being considered by Congress, is actually responsive to the needs of LGBT workers. In fact, the current version of ENDA prohibits the government from gathering data about the numbers of lesbian and gay people in the workforce and it sharply limits the ability of workers to seek redress for harassment.

Data on the lived experience of LGBT workers are sparse but growing. Pioneering efforts to identify wage disparities between gay and non-gay workers has helped us understand some of the realities of LGBT workers. Few studies have sought to gather data about the discriminatory behavior of employers. The first large-scale audit of employment discrimination in the United States took place in 2005. A researcher sent pairs of fictitious resumes to employers in response to 1,769 job postings in seven states (similar audits have been conducted in Canada and

Austria). All resumes were from college seniors listing experience that would be considered equally valued from the perspective of the relevant labor markets. Half of the applicants' resumes had some sort of indication that the applicant was gay. For example, if the post were for a job dealing with finances, the resume might list that the candidate had been a treasurer for a gay group. In total, the resumes resulted in over 300 call-backs. The results indicated that the resumes from gay applicants were forty percent less likely to receive a call-back.[17]

The findings of the study have complex policy implications. If these applicants were real, it is highly unlikely that they would have known they were being passed over because of bias. They would not have filed a complaint under a non-discrimination law, and if they had they probably would not have been able to prove anything. What LGBT people should have is the capability to work in a productive and satisfying way. Equality laws, by themselves, do not provide that.

One of the most memorable calls I ever received at the Center was from a gay man in a rural but highly populated area of Pennsylvania. He was being ruthlessly harassed on the job after a coworker outed him at work. He had advanced through the ranks at his job for a few years, and he was getting a decent salary, but after the outing everything changed. Coworkers mocked him or went silent, his boss stopped inviting him to workplace social events, his assignments started drying up, and he was isolated in the office. He was desperate to keep his job, but the situation was becoming intolerable. He told me he was calling from his car in the parking lot in front of the building where he worked. He was lying down on the front seat of his car with his cell phone so that no one would see him cry.

His prospects for comparable employment elsewhere were low. His family was tired of hearing him talk about his problems and would provide no support. He lived in his boyfriend's apartment, but the relationship was unraveling. There were no local LGBT support programs. There was no directly relevant law to protect this man, though we talked about some alternative tactics and remedies. Frankly, even if there had been a law to prohibit what was happening at his workplace, this man didn't need a lawsuit. He needed a job.

What *Romer v. Evans* accomplished in an immediate sense was to permit towns and counties in Colorado to adopt local equality laws. Municipal and county ordinances prohibiting discrimination have been a goal of LGBT advocates in Colorado and many other states. In states and cities where the LGBT community has achieved political influence, LGBT advocates have sought these laws as public symbols of support for LGBT people, as well as tools to respond to anti-LGBT bias of employers.

The reality of these laws does not live up to their promise. Decades of experience with equal rights laws for women and racial minorities inform us of the limitations of these legal standards. I know from working at the US Equal Employment Opportunity Commission that the system to enforce such laws is often unfriendly, back-logged, and expensive. Workers with legitimate claims end up with just that—a good claim, but no job.

A 2011 study concluded that state-level anti-discrimination laws had a positive effect on the earnings of gay men.[18] The effect was not as strong with regard to non-white gay men, and such laws had little effect on the earnings of lesbians. Local laws did not seem to have any significant effect. These laws are necessary, but they cannot remove the barriers faced by LGBT people on a day-to-day basis.

-2-

Choosing Goals

If legal equality is not sufficient to achieve the good lives that all people deserve, then what is? Concluding that equality is insufficient is the easy part. However, that conclusion does not form the basis for a movement. Except for those whose jobs involve political and social criticism, no one ever rallied under a banner of "We Have A Critique." Social movement theory, as well as any successful political activist, tells us a movement needs to have a clear purpose. The LGBT movement needs to be deliberate in its choice of post-equality movement priorities.

I am going to explore two reasons for the need for deliberation. First, progressives, including those in the LGBT movement, have frequently found themselves bottlenecked by an inability to articulate a clear, affirmative vision. The lack of "the vision thing" has been a historical blur on the ability of the Democrats to keep the White House. Al Gore and John Kerry mumbled their way to defeat. The 2012 presidential election was a lesson in winning by taking a stance. Barack Obama projected an early and clear message and pounced on Mitt Romney's floppiness.

The 1993 LGBT March on Washington was hugely successful because of its heretofore-unseen turnout of a million people. In part, this was due to its platform, which, although a bit of a kitchen sink, was prominent in the minds of the community. Groups at every level had spent a year discussing it, fighting about it, and getting their piece of it. Everyone knew enough about it to have an opinion. Subsequent marches were powerful events as well, but the lack of energy around a strong vision dampened turnout and impact. The march in 2000 lacked appeal beyond those already engaged in the agenda of the Human Rights Campaign, the organization that sponsored it. The platform of the 2009 march seemed to be cut and pasted from the list of complaints the community had about its expectations of the Obama administration.

Legal equality is a powerful vision because it is clear and simple. If the movement wants to expand its vision beyond achieving legal equality, it must have an equally clear vision about where it is going. The vision that I propose – that of achieving a good life for LGBT people –

must be articulated with clarity in order to be understandable and politically useful.

Defining a good life is no small task. Debates over the meaning of a good life have occupied everyone from ancient philosophers to televangelists to presidential candidates. The term 'good life' carries with it a long history of argument and research on the meaning of well-being, happiness, and worthiness in one's life. Aristotle spent a lifetime refining the concept of *eudaimonia* (Greek for "good life"). Henry David Thoreau connected a good life to nature. Even Rick Warren has pitched in with his proposition that fulfillment comes from a purpose-driven life based on knowing God's purpose for us and carrying out his mission. LGBT people must provide their own vision of a good life.

I use the term 'better life' rather than 'good life' to communicate essentially the same thing. The phrase 'good life' does not translate well into the contemporary American political context. It sounds either too moralizing or too much like a dance song. The term 'better life' also recognizes that the task is not just to seek one preferred way to live, but to improve lives even when those improvements do not result in transcendent perfection. A better life is something that is achievable and actionable. As a movement with many different kinds of organizations, staking a claim on a clear vision of a better life helps draw people together for group action and collective goals.

The second reason for needing a deliberate approach to post-equality movement priorities is to avoid being mainstreamed into invisibility and reinforcing the same barriers experienced by non-LGBT people. If we step back and look at the larger sweep of history, we see society has been attempting to articulate a good life for LGBT people all along, sometimes proposing that jail, medical treatment or spiritual redemption would serve LGBT people best. LGBT people now have more control over the agenda than ever before. The equality agenda is just one phase in a larger path of progress for LGBT people. In its most formal sense, equality gives us the right to be treated equally as well or as badly as everyone else. An equally bad life is not the end point of the LGBT movement. The vision must capture the notion of progress for LGBT people toward a better life.

Many groups have already reviewed their mission statements and adopted missions that are based on what I call a post-equality agenda. For example, Funders for LGBT Issues, an organization that promotes LGBT philanthropy, recently adopted a mission statement that expanded its focus beyond equality:

> Funders for LGBTQ Issues seeks to mobilize philanthropic resources that enhance the well-being of lesbian, gay, bisexual, transgender, and queer communities, promote equity, and advance racial, economic, and gender justice.[19]

Inevitably, the movement will look to its next tasks seeking better lives for LGBT people.

I will walk through some of the approaches to sexual orientation and gender identity that we have seen in America in the past century. The history of sexuality in America is rich with stories of struggle and advancement. I do not intend to review that history here. Rather, I chose particular historical perspectives as examples of how American society responded to LGBT people.

Each approach has incorporated a set of beliefs about what a good life was meant to be. Some approaches viewed deviation from gender norms as evil, and a better life required conversion or elimination of the gender deviant and invert. Some approaches concentrated on the psychology of anti-LGBT people and on how a better life could be achieved by confronting intergroup conflict. Currently, many advocates focus on the problems caused by institutions that treat LGBT people differently than non-LGBT people. For those advocates, changing institutions is a means to a better life.

Each of these successive approaches has embraced an increasingly empowered vision of LGBT people. After laying out past perspectives of LGBT people, I propose a new set of perspectives. I argue that we should adopt a vision of LGBT people, and their lives, which affirms their goodness and moral worth.

Curing LGBT People

The view that homosexuality and gender deviance is a disease has been promoted by professionals and advocates throughout American history. For those who held this view, the path to a better life was to cure the disease and live life free of any impulse to deviate from gender and sexual norms. Charles Silverstein, a therapist and writer on issues of psychology, lists the cure methods that have been attempted by medical professionals:

- Surgically transplanting testicular cells from a heterosexual man into the testes of a gay man.
- Castration
- Implanting stereotaxic leads into the brain of a gay man
- Cerebral ablation (removing part of the brain)
- Androgen replacement
- Aversive conditioning using electrical, chemical, and covert techniques
- Hypnosis
- Psychoanalysis[20]

The intensity of concern exhibited by governments and cultural leaders over matters of sex and gender reflects the power that these matters have in each person's life. This power is revealed most brutally by the fact that the people undergoing the procedures listed above did so voluntarily. These represent the many people whose vision of a better life includes eradicating homosexuality or gender-nonconformity from their life, sometimes employing methods that are cruel and desperate.

CATEGORIZING PEOPLE. The sexuality and gender of humans is extraordinarily diverse. The alphabet soup label "LGBT" is indicative of the historical variations of sexual orientation and gender identity. The term "homosexual" itself did not exist until the late 1800s, when sexologists began writing on the subject. During that time a small number of writers in the medical field began publishing books and articles proposing categories for sexual functions and hypotheses as to origins and causes of various sexual desires, personality types, and behaviors. German physician Magnus Hirschfeld, himself openly homosexual, wrote about homosexuality, transexualism, and transvestism, and was the first to advocate for the rights of homosexuals and transsexuals.[21]

Hirschfeld's work became familiar to Harry Benjamin, a German physician who left Germany in 1913 and eventually moved to San Francisco. Benjamin worked with individuals whose gender expression or perception of themselves did not match their sex at birth. He began providing hormone treatment to transsexuals in the late 1940s. In 1952, one of Benjamin's patients, an American GI named George Jorgensen, underwent surgery in Sweden and returned to New York as Christine Jorgensen. Her transition was featured on the front page of the New York Daily News, and she became an instant celebrity.

The high level of publicity surrounding Jorgensen's transition led to more people seeking medical attention.[22]

The work of Alfred Kinsey around the same period received even more publicity. During the late 1940s and early 1950s, Kinsey and several others at Indiana University conducted in-person interviews with thousands of people and issued a series of high profile reports. He proposed a scale of sexual experience and response that placed hetero- and homosexuality within the same continuum from zero to six. A six is someone who is exclusively homosexual, and a zero is someone who is exclusively heterosexual. The continuum reaffirmed divisions between hetero- and homosexuality, but acknowledged the diversity of desires along the same continuum. Kinsey also stressed the variations between behavior and feeling. It is his reports that popularized the belief that ten percent of the population is homosexual.[23]

Kinsey's scale did not describe expressions or feelings about gender. In the early 1960s, the first gender clinic in the United States was opened. Its focus was treating children who deviated from the gender assigned at birth and reinforcing gender conformity. A few years later, Dr. Benjamin published *The Transsexual Phenomenon,* which made distinctions between homosexuality, transsexuality, and transvestism. He also described an affirmative standard of care for transsexuals, which has been updated by the World Professional Association for Transgender Health (formerly the Harry Benjamin Association).[24]

However, the supportive views of Dr. Benjamin did not reflect the mainstream view of the American medical community. In a survey of 400 physicians in the 1960s, doctors were asked about how they would respond to a request by a 30-year-old male seeking sex reassignment surgery, where that individual was happier living as female, was attracted to men, and had undergone two years of psychotherapy and been deemed ready for the surgery by the treating psychiatrist. Eight percent of the respondents considered the person 'severely neurotic,' and fifteen percent considered him 'psychotic.'[25]

DIAGNOSING DISEASE. The American medical establishment formalized its own categorizations of diseases in the early 1950s. The *Diagnostic and Statistical Manual of Mental Disorders* (DSM) is the primary guide used by health practitioners in the United States for defining mental disorders. When the American Psychiatric Association (APA) published the first edition of the DSM in 1952, homosexuality was included in the category of Sociopathic Personality Disorders.[26] In the second version (DSM-II), published in 1968, homosexuality was included with sexual perversions such as pedophilia, sadism, and fetishism.[27] A better life, from a medical perspective, meant treating and ridding a person of these disorders.

Gay and lesbian advocates sought to question this approach to providing a better life. In an effort to get the APA to consider the wealth of research that demonstrated homosexuality was not a disease, a number of gay and lesbian activists disrupted the 1970 and 1971 annual conferences. This led to the removal of homosexuality from the DSM-II by the APA Board of Trustees, followed by a final action by the full membership of the APA in 1974.[28]

Although homosexuality has been depathologized, the notion of homosexuality as a disease persists. Many therapists will engage in therapy to help clients decrease their homosexual preferences and behaviors. Conservatives use the tactic of portraying non-heterosexual sex as a pathology. The APA still pathologizes "paraphilia," defined as non-normative sexual behavior. The conservative group Concerned Women for America argued in the Supreme Court that acceptance of homosexuality would lead to acceptance of other non-normative paraphilias. In a legal brief submitted to the Supreme Court by Concerned Women for America in *Lawrence v. Texas*, the group argued:

> [T]he Court should remain unwilling to go down a road that would inevitably lead the Court to face equal protection claims raised by individuals who engage in other types of sexual conduct (paraphilias), such as pedophilia or zoophilia, which some characterize as a "sexual orientation." It is conceivable that the paraphilias…, which are presently classified as "mental disorders" will be declassified just as the American Psychiatric Association declassified homosexuality as a "mental disorder" in 1973.[29]

In the early 1980s, the next two *Diagnostic and Statistical Manual of Mental Disorders* (DSM-III and III-R) were published with several diagnoses relevant to gender identity (transsexualism, gender identity disorder of childhood, and gender identity disorder of adolescence and adulthood).[30] In 1994, the diagnoses were collapsed into one overarching diagnosis of gender identity disorder, with different criteria for adults, adolescents, and children.

The World Health Organization (WHO) maintains the International Classification of Diseases (ICD), used by most insurance companies, governments, and medical communities outside of the United States. In 2015, the WHO will finalize its first revision of the ACD since 1990. The classification issued in 1990 included five variations of psychopathologies related to gender identity. Today, the discussions no longer focus on misconceptions and controversy. Rather, the concerns are the need to find a balance between the stigmatization of medical disorders and the need for diagnostic categories in order to facilitate access to healthcare. On the one hand, some activists oppose the identification of gender identities in a document that is about disorders. On the other, recognition in the ICD is the basis for insurance and medical coverage in many countries. The WHO will ultimately be the arbiter of these competing concerns when it issues the final revisions in 2015.

POLITICS AND SICKNESS. Conservatives have portrayed homosexuality and gender non-conformity as not merely diseases but as diseases that remove a person's ability to use any of their faculties and intelligence, thus disqualifying them from participation as full citizens. The "Lavender Scare" in the 1950s used homosexuals as scapegoats for a strategy to increase political anxiety and gain support for government security measures. In 1958, a congressional committee discussed the employment of homosexuals and issued a report entitled, *The Employment of Homosexuals and Other Sex Perverts in the US Government.* This report equates homosexuality with a personality disorder stating, "Psychiatric physicians are generally agreed that indulgence in sexually perverted practices indicates a personality which has failed to reach sexual maturity."[31]

Supreme Court Justice William Rehnquist relied on the notion of homosexuality as a disorder in a case in which a university had denied recognition of a gay student group. The university argued that homosexual acts, at the time of its decision, were still criminalized in several states. Rehnquist analyzed the decision of the university and based his analysis on an analogy to quarantining infectious people.

> From the point of view of the University, however, the question is more akin to whether those suffering from measles have a constitutional right, in violation of quarantine regulations, to associate together and with others who do not

presently have measles, in order to urge repeal of a state law providing that measles sufferers be quarantined.[32]

Catholic teachings hold that homosexual acts are "intrinsically disordered".[33] These teachings indicates that the tendency toward homosexuality is a moral evil that disqualifies a person from affective maturity and disables their ability to relate correctly to men and women. Yet, homosexuality is not inherent. For the disorder there is a cure. Catholic policy recognizes the possibility of recovery, as long as three years have passed without homosexual acts or attachments to gay culture.[34]

In the late 1990s, conservatives upped their emphasis on the disease model of homosexuality by mounting a massive publicity campaign to push conversion therapy. "The truth will set you free" campaign bought full-page ads in major newspapers in order to portray this therapy as their version of the better life. A picture of a woman with the caption "I'm living proof that truth can set you free" appeared above a block of text. The text told the woman's story, beginning with her youth as an insecure girl with problems of sexual exploitation, lack of information, a desire to have loving family relationships, and vulnerability toward other women who cared. That girl ended up being drawn into a lesbian life, a bad life of violence and disorder and isolation.[35]

The ads were part of efforts by the ex-gay movement to promote a two-pronged message. First was the claim that therapy could turn a gay person straight. Second, related to this self-healing model, was the implicit message that discrimination suffered by LGBT people was their own fault. If people were not making the effort to better their own lives by eliminating homosexuality, then they did not deserve protections. The key to a better life, said the woman in the ads, was having freed herself from homosexuality and devoted herself to her gender role, her husband, and God. The key to a better life for society was for LGBT people everywhere to do the same.

In 2012, conservatives used the image of the out-of-control, predatory cross-dresser to defeat an Anchorage, Alaska, ballot initiative that would have prohibited discrimination based on sexual orientation and gender identity. In the last few weeks before the election, anti-gay groups ran television ads featuring a cartoon figure of a male lumberjack in a dress working at a daycare center. Rhetoric of the right-wing campaign focused on the specter of having to hire and work with transvestites. The ballot initiative, which initially had strong support, lost by a large margin after the initiative's opponents invoked these images.

Curing Homophobia

As more LGBT people came to accept their own sexuality and gender identity, the notion of a better life shifted. Whereas under the disease model the homosexual was the source of the problem, subsequent ways of seeing homosexuality placed the source of concern with those who acted out of prejudice and stigma.

The homophile movement marked one of the first moments of this shift. Communities formed in bars and living rooms, where activists gathered for mutual support and discussion. Some historians credit World War II with an increase in same-sex intimacy in the mid-century, as men were mobilized for the war and demobilized in coastal cities such as San Francisco and New York and women entered the labor force to take jobs opened up by the wartime economy. Others have focused on the process of urbanization and industrialization in the early 1900s, which increased the options for people to live autonomous lives and decreased the necessity of engaging in sexual relationships for the sake of local economic production.[36] For a variety of reasons, the homophile movement began claiming its voice in mid-century America.

In November 1950, Harry Hay founded the Mattachine Society in Los Angeles. The name was taken from a secret French society of masked men. The group was organized so that participants could use pseudonyms. Only the leaders were known to one another. Mattachines avoided visibility and social prominence. Philosophically, the Mattachines sought accommodation, believing themselves to be like heterosexuals in every way except for the fact that they had sex with men. The mission of the homophile movement was to educate gay and lesbian people about the oppression they faced and to work to end their oppression in a manner consistent with the highest ethics of the society around them. Their tactic in reaching the better life was self-awareness, mutual support, daily problem solving, and constantly reminding themselves of their own worth.

In the late 1950s, Del Martin and Phyllis Lyon founded the Daughters of Bilitis (DOB) in San Francisco as an alternative to bars, which were often raided by police. The politics of the DOB generally reflected the politics of the Mattachine society, as well as the mutual support model of the emerging feminist movement. The DOB had chapters across the country with the mission to promote "the integration of the homosexual into society." The group began publishing and distributing the newsletter *The Ladder*. The DOB formed the groundwork for a lesbian movement.[37]

The Homosexual in America, an influential book by Daniel Webster Corey, described the homosexual in a way that echoed the American values of privacy and liberty. Cory sought to normalize homosexuality and locate the sexual minority struggle within the African-American civil rights movement. That movement was based on the principle that individuals may have certain characteristics, for example skin color, that were not relevant to the individual's value as a worker, voter, leader, or citizen. Homosexuality, like skin color, meant merely that the homosexual would be as fit or as flawed as anyone else. Corey criticized the selection bias by the medical community inherent to its pathologization of homosexuality. He suggested that psychiatrists only saw homosexuals as patients who were frustrated and maladjusted:

> What the homosexual wants is freedom—not only freedom of expression, but also sexual freedom. By sexual freedom is meant the right of any person to gratify his urges when and how he sees fit, without fear of social consequences, so long as he does not use force of either violence, threats or superior age; so long as he does not inflict bodily harm or disease upon another person; so long as the other person is of sound mind and agrees to the activity.[38]

Activists shifted from accommodation to protest by staging the first national protest in 1965, when a dozen activists picketed in front of the White House. These protests were followed by "reminder marches" each July in front of Independence Hall in Philadelphia. Ironically, when the homophile groups began their marches in 1965, they continued to avoid articulating an independent set of gay values. The goal of the marches was to present gay people in a manner that was utterly non-threatening. Pictures of women in smart skirts and men in coats and ties solemnly marching in a circle holding neatly printed signs have become iconic images of queer history.

Years later, the LGBT community refined its articulation of the problem when it began using the term "homophobia" and, later, the term "transphobia." Psychoanalyst George Weinberg, credited for the term in the early 1970s, first used it to signify the dread of being in close quarters with a homosexual:

> I coined the word homophobia to mean it was a phobia about homosexuals.... It was a fear of homosexuals which seemed associated with a fear of contagion, a fear of reducing the things one fought for—home and family. It was a religious fear and it had led to great brutality as fear always does.[39]

Similarly, advocates have used the term "transphobia" to refer to prejudice and bias against transgender people. Both of these terms have served not only as labels for anti-gay and anti-trans people, but also as labels for rules requiring non-LGBT people to conform to gender norms. Men are not supposed to show affection. Women are not supposed to show independence. The popularization of the concepts of homophobia and transphobia helped draw a circle around bad people and bad policies, and congealed a politically pro-gay vision of the better life. The better life thus meant eliminating homophobia and transphobia and the resulting damage they caused

LGBT people. Social conservative and former US Representative William Dannemeyer, in his book on the topic, noted that homophobia shifts the debate away from the claim

> ...that homosexuals are disturbed people by saying that it is those who disapprove of them who are mentally unbalanced, that they are in the grips of a 'phobia.' The term gay is also a positive reference to homosexuality. ...[T]he use of the two in tandem has had a profound effect on the dialogue concerning these crucial issues and has tipped the scales, perhaps irreversibly, in favor of the homosexuals.[40]

In December 2012, the Associated Press banned the use of the word "homophobia" from its style manual on the grounds that it has become associated with a mental disability. The AP now opts for the term "anti-gay." The AP is not a medical organization. Nevertheless, the AP's action shows the vast change in attitude about homosexuality from thirty years earlier when the debate was whether homosexuality itself was a mental disability. George Weinberg himself opposes the ban, noting that homophobia is an irrational fear causing distress to the person experiencing it, and being anti-gay is simply having negative thoughts or feeling about gay people.[41] Other psychologists have refined homophobia into different categories of sexual stigma and prejudice. Regardless, the notion that the barrier to a better life lies not with homosexuality and gender-nonconformity, but with prejudice and stigma, is one that has been successfully promulgated.

I witnessed this shift during my own coming out process. In a very typical story, I came home from college one weekend, and my mother asked me about one of my male friends. The relationship seemed "more than just friends" to her. I told her I was gay. She said, "Well, we will find you a therapist to help you avoid this." I said I was not going to do that. Without skipping much of a beat she said, "Then I need to find myself a therapist to figure out how to deal with this." I was lucky to have a mother who easily pivoted away from the notion that I was sick. She was supportive of me and my work in gay rights from that moment on.

The gay men and drag queens who resisted police crackdowns at New York's Stonewall Inn in June of 1969 brought strength and visibility to a new gay liberation movement. One can debate whether liberationists constitute a distinct movement or are just a more visible component of the growing number of LGBT people. What can be said was that organizations such as the Gay Liberation Front took a different stance on homosexuality than the homophile movement. Liberationists questioned the gender rules that applied to everyone, not just gay people.

Raising consciousness was an important objective of the liberationists, one they shared with rapidly growing lesbian empowerment and feminist movements. Liberationists joined with women, African-Americans, Latinos, and Native Americans to challenge and question rules about sex and family. The relationship between the body and nature was tied to questions of the environment and property. The ability to make decisions about one's own body was tied to the ability to participate in collective policymaking. The relevance (or irrelevance) of sex, the body, and race to issues of work and politics and family were prominent. Coming out was an important part of well-being and activism, though only as much as it increased people's options and freedoms. A rigid gay identity was not the goal. Whereas homophiles would say "gay is good," liberationists would say "gay is good for everyone." For liberationists, the better life included the ability for everyone to authentically live and express their inner sense of sexuality and gender identity.

Accepting Difference

Many leading voices in the LGBT community continue to follow a liberationist agenda and seek social justice that liberates people from the limiting rules of gender and sexuality. For others, the liberationist agenda's lack of political traction does not offer a path to a better life. A gay rights movement emerged in the seventies based on a desire to obtain civil protections that already existed for other protected classes. At that time the historic Civil Rights Act of 1964[42] was making its mark, and a growing economy was presenting opportunities for changes in the workplace and schools. This gay civil rights movement sought to model gay advocacy on the black civil rights movement.

The emphasis on liberating the sexuality and gender of all people shifted to protecting a non-conforming identity for the minority of people who acknowledged it in themselves. The new model was less threatening in that it did not seek to have all Americans question their own sexuality and gender. Raising each person's consciousness of oppression was no longer the primary tactic. As one leading psychologist on sexual orientation prejudice said, the "implication of this change is that such [anti-gay] attitudes can be understood in terms of intergroup conflicts rather than intrapsychic conflicts."[43] The term "homophobia," originally coined to refer to an individual's reaction to another individual, was now applied to government policies, organizations, and political positions.

This model promoted the development of separate identities and threw LGBT people more deeply into the dynamics of identity politics that permeates the American civil rights movements. People are categorized according to a particular characteristic, and then one category of people is compared to another. Government action is judged according to whether (and why) one group is treated better than another. This basic formula is found in courts, political processes, and cultural discussions. In this dynamic, lesbians, gay men, bisexuals, and transgender people have each developed their own separate communities and sub-communities with goals that sometimes conflict and sometimes coincide.

In order for LGBT people to avail themselves of the protections in place for blacks and women, LGBT people would have to adopt the narrative that homosexuality and gender identity are innate. The template of the civil rights movement included the assumption that innate individual characteristics—race, sex, national origin—were immutable. Though religion is chosen as well, it has always been seen as rooted so deeply in personal identity that one should not be put in the position of giving it up. The LGBT rights movement adopted the reasoning that people are just born that way.

The "born this way" argument has personal resonance. We all see toddlers express gendered behavior. Many

LGBT people commonly experience the feeling that their sexual orientation and gender identity is innate. Whether the source of that feeling is something that is in place at birth or something powerful that occurs during the child development process is still debatable. The attachment to the immutability of homosexuality is not universal.

I remember attending a meeting in Stockholm, Sweden, where a cabinet-level government official was speaking about sexuality and health. He related a story about a conversation he had with his adolescent daughter about her sexual choices. He told her that she should be mindful and responsible about sex and that she should always assume she has full control over how and with whom she would have sex, including whether it was with a man or woman. Both were equally valid, and he did not see much point in getting too wrapped up in figuring out whether the creator had made her a lesbian or a straight woman. I remember reflexively looking around the room to see if press were there to cover his statements before remembering that we were not in the US, where such a statement would damage a politician's career. In Stockholm, no one seemed to be highly concerned with whether people were "born this way."

Many LGBT people talk about a time when they were young and they began to feel they were different, further reinforcing the notion that sexual orientation and gender identity was something that happened early in our identity development. In recent years, the acceptability of a fluid sexuality (in large part because of the success of the LGBT and women's movements) has provided more space for people to question this. Aaron Swartz, the young computer genius credited with the invention of RSS code and prosecuted for hacking MIT's academic database, wrote about his own life at age 23:

> Having sex with someone shouldn't require an identity crisis. (Nobody sees having-sex-with-white-people as part of their identity, even if that's primarily who they're attracted to.) If we truly want to expand the scope of human freedom, we should encourage people to date who they want; not just provide more categorical boxes for them to slot themselves into. A man who has mostly dated men should be just as welcome to date women as a woman who's mostly dated men. So that's why I'm not gay. I hook up with people. I enjoy it. Sometimes they're men, sometimes they're women. I don't see why it needs to be any more complicated than that.[44]

For Swartz and the thoughtful government official in Stockholm, the identity-based structure of the US LGBT movement may not make much sense. Their statements support a view of a better life that is free from boundaries and barriers of identity. Relationships are based on consent, responsibility, and choice.

Swartz did hit on a hot-button issue in the US: sex. Where sex arises in discussions of LGBT rights, advocates are careful to try to mute its prominence and take the heat off. Many advocates for decriminalization of sodomy have been careful to argue that they are not supportive of reform of other regulations of sexuality.[45] Images of same-sex married couples are contextualized to carefully avoid raising uncomfortable questions about the sexual lives of lesbians and gay men. Sexual freedom generally does not appear in the movement agenda.

The petitioners in *Lawrence v. Texas,* for example, argued that the sodomy law interfered with a right to private associational conduct.[46] To the extent that differences between gays and straights were undeniable and visible, the gay rights movement has sought tolerance. Knowing that there was an official state sexuality—heterosexuality—LGBT people sought a stable peace between the accepted majority and the homosexual minority. The Supreme Court opinion in *Romer v. Evans*, which overturned Colorado's Amendment 2, said that the country must tolerate, not hate, lesbian and gay people. However, the boundary between gay and straight, center and margin, us and them, remains clear, and it is defined by sexual behavior.[47]

In an effort to minimize the significance of the boundary and claim equality protections available to other groups, some gay rights advocates have portrayed gay identities in ways that would trigger empathy and alliance-building (we are good workers, we are innocent victims of hate crimes, we are economically screwed cohabitants, we are consumers in an uncaring medical system). LGBT leaders have actively avoided showcasing identities that threaten the right (we find love outside of traditional families, we find support in created communities of choice, we have sex for the purpose of joy rather than procreation). The policy goal became assimilation for the purpose of obtaining benefits enjoyed by others, and although these groups have achieved success on a variety of levels, earning that success has required gay sex to remain in the closet while leaders sought to find a place for homosexuality within larger accepted cultural norms.

Living Better Lives

Legal Equality Doesn't Mean Lived Equality

Changing the institutions that oppress LGBT people is necessary, but it is not the goal. Institutions are a means to an end. The goal of the movement is to improve the lives of people. As a student at George Washington University in the late eighties, I found myself in the center of my first institutional change campaign after a series of anti-gay incidents on campus. The University had refused to adopt a non-discrimination policy even though the law in the District of Columbia already prohibited discrimination based on sexual orientation. Officials feared such a policy would threaten the University's relationship with the Reserve Officers Training Corps program, and the associated tens of millions of dollars in federal income.

I organized students and alumni, and Law Professor Mary Cheh (now a member of the District of Columbia City Council) was the primary advocate in the faculty senate. She was the hero of many students for many reasons, not the least of which was convincing the faculty senate to pass a resolution in favor of the policy. University President Stephen Trachtenberg repeatedly refused to meet with us. I remember walking with Professor Cheh back from the President's office after he had skipped out on a promised appointment. She was outraged and was having a professorial rant right there on the sidewalk in front of the student center. She asked me, "Why aren't you outraged, too?" I remember saying, "There is only one direction this can go. We will get there." I also remember thinking how great she was for maintaining her outrage and calling me out for not maintaining mine.

In order to get a meeting with President Trachtenberg, the students finally purchased a lunch with him at a fundraising auction held to benefit the National Association of Public Interest Law (now Equal Justice Works). We invited other University officials and let President Trachtenberg know a couple weeks beforehand who was going to show up and what the agenda was going to be. He felt ambushed and trapped, and he negotiated a bizarre choreography of what could and could not be discussed at the lunch as a condition of his attendance.

Held at a very formal private dining club, the lunch conversation was polite and academic. During the lunch, one of the deans from his office asked, "What is the long-term aim of your movement? Generations from now, when you have equality and you are not controversial, will a group like the gay and lesbian student group be just like a Scottish gaming club?" The question silenced me. I had no answer. After we get all the equality we want, what is next? I mumbled back, "Sure, just like a Scottish gaming club." I thought to myself, "Whatever, let's wait until that happens and we can talk more about it then."

A Scottish gaming club? I gave a convenient, but wrong answer. LGBT people are different than non-LGBT people. Some of those differences do not matter any more than being in a Scottish gaming club. Some matter a great deal. Same-sex couples have sex differently, which should not matter to those who are not having it. It should matter to those who are. Should it matter to a doctor? Sometimes, yes. LGBT people have different kinds of families. That should not matter to the person who sells them groceries, but it should matter to the person who sells them life insurance. Other differences are created by stigma. The persistent driver of the continued needs of LGBT people, even after full legal equality, is the fact that LGBT people will continue to live their lives and face unique challenges and opportunities.

The University adopted the policy a few weeks after our meeting with the President. The policies of George

Washington University are now quite LGBT friendly. Married same-sex couples are treated as any other married couple for purposes of University housing and benefits; LGB people serve in the Officer Training Corps; employment discrimination is prohibited; fraternities that do not admit homosexuals have been kicked off campus; openly gay faculty members are media darlings. Nevertheless, there are still LGBT students harassed out of their dorms and straight students being teased by the term "faggot," faculty members who dare not be too out before they get tenure, and students who struggle to re-closet themselves when it comes time to apply for jobs. And the school continues to be expensive, tries to be exclusive, and succeeds in being mostly white in a city that is mostly not.

The persistence of discrimination after passage of equality laws is a clear indicator of their limitations. The Equal Pay Act of 1963[48] sought to equalize wages between men and women. After four decades, women still make 77 cents on the dollar.[49] The Fair Housing Act of 1968[50] was passed one week after the assassination of Martin Luther King, Jr., yet African-Americans continue to be denied rental and mortgage opportunities in a systemic fashion.

The Civil Rights Act of 1964[51] outlaws employment discrimination based on a number of factors. Nonetheless, patterns of bias in labor markets persist. That law works very well for those cases of discrimination where there is proof of bias. In my work at the US Equal Employment Opportunity Commission, I prosecuted a series of cases against high-end restaurants. In one case, only men were permitted to serve during the lucrative lunch hour and women during the lower-volume dinner hour. The discrimination was obvious, and these cases were not difficult to win.

At the same time that discrimination has become less tolerated within our society, its presence is becoming more subtle and insidious. Later in my career, I represented a young man at a manufacturing plant. My client was not fired, but he was subjected to a series of acts of bias. My client began getting excluded from casual discussions where overtime opportunities would be revealed. He had to work with older equipment that was assigned to him. Notices for promotion would not come to his attention as he was subtly excluded from interactions. Slowly, his pay trajectory altered. The discriminatory act was hard to pin down. There was no "smoking gun." After several levels of hearings and appeals, the court held that the evidence was insufficient for him to win his case.

As minorities become legally mainstreamed by equal protection laws, discrimination also moves from the outside to the inside of cultural dynamics. Employers, teachers, and leaders learn the new legal rules surrounding discrimination. Bias becomes more intertwined with mainstream decision making and less vulnerable to exposure. The goal of obtaining rights may leave out the necessity to confront underlying social and cultural marginalization. Urvashi Vaid, former executive director of the National Gay and Lesbian Task Force and former president of the Arcus Foundation, calls this goal "Virtual Equality" in her book by the same name. In what is the most exhaustive accounting of the movement ever written, she draws some broad lessons:

> What gay political history illustrates is that a rights-oriented movement can coexist with prejudice with lesbians and gay men. It can even advance while leaving homophobia intact. This is possible because civil rights can be won without displacing the moral and sexual hierarchy that enforces antigay stigmatization: you do not have to recognize the fundamental humanity of gay people in order to agree that they should be treated equally and fairly under the law.[52]

I would like to examine the operation of stigma and prejudice, first looking at larger cultural patterns and understanding how stigma and prejudice operate in the minds of individuals who carry negative and false stereotypes about LGBT people. Then, I will shift attention from culture to the individual to look at the lived experience of LGBT people. I look at the path that individuals follow and the obstacles that individuals face as they complete this path. The successful completion of the path to full human development is the goal of the proposals in this book. In the final chapter in the book, I also argue that the experiences of LGBT people give rise to a unique understanding of civic values held by many Americans. Each person's path to full human development is unique. Nonetheless, LGBT people can claim a distinctive understanding of these values which is grounded in having to negotiate and respond to prejudice, stigma, rejection and powerlessness. The starting point is understanding the context in which LGBT people live.

LIVING UNDER STIGMA. Even after LGBT people obtain legal equality, society will still have a culture that is divided along lines of in/out, majority/minority, the preferred/disfavored. I will discuss each side of this equation, first looking at how stigma and prejudice operate to guide the preferences of some, then looking at how these preferences limit the options of LGBT people in everyday life.

The decision to treat someone differently, ignore someone, or prefer someone is based on many factors, the least of which is legal requirements. It is not simply the freaked out homophobes on one side and the LGBT-loving people on the other. Psychologist Gregory Herek suggests a fuller view of how to look at these dynamics. With many alterations (my apologies to Professor Herek), what I set out here is taken from his work.[53] The starting point for these dynamics is stigma. Stigma is a shared belief about an attribute. For example, the attribute might be wearing a turban. Many people might share a belief that a man wearing a turban is anti-American. The attribute might be a thick southern accent. Many people might share a belief that the person is uneducated. Stigma assigns meaning to an otherwise meaningless attribute. A turban means political beliefs. A drawl means academic achievement.

Sexual stigma is the belief that someone with a particular sexuality is inferior. Gender identity stigma is a belief that someone who expresses their gender in a particular way is inferior. Sexual and gender identity stigma each engulfs the entire identity of an LGBT person who is stigmatized. A transgender person is considered too untrustworthy to be an accountant or assumed to be too out of control to be a suitable tenant. Stigma is the group version of jumping to conclusions.

Prejudice is the dynamic, or process of prejudgment, that occurs in the head of an individual when they apply a stigma. Sexual prejudice is the enduring negative attitude toward a social group—in this case, homosexuals. Gender identity prejudice is the same, applied toward someone who does not conform to traditional gender roles. Both sexual and gender identity prejudice can operate at the same time, and often the lesbian, gay, or bisexual person is disfavored because they have also violated gender roles. Differentiating the two is not easy, but certainly homosexuality is becoming decoupled from gender nonconforming expression. Visibly conforming masculine gay men (think of the many sports figures who have come out), and feminine lesbians (think *The L Word*) still face antipathy. The metrosexual and the straight sissy also face antipathy. Both sexual and gender prejudice can exist in the minds of LGBT people and result in stratification and ill treatment within the community.

CONVERT, HIDE/PRETEND, AND DOWN-PLAY/PASS.

Prejudice and stigma can impose unwritten requirements on LGBT people. As LGBT people go to work, attend school, engage with friends, and face personal ups and downs, stigma and prejudice place pressures on them to alter their behavior and identity. Many of these demands exist even when LGBT people have legal equality. Law professor Kenji Yoshino explains three types of demands that are made of LGBT people by society and institutions.[54] Though I use different terminology, I take these explanations from Yoshino's work.

The first and most strident demand is to convert. Basically, this occurs when an LGBT person is told to stop being LGBT. Convert from gay to ex-gay. Sodomy laws were harsh instructions from the government to convert. Teenagers are still instructed by family, church, and therapists to convert. According to his testimony in the trial against California's Proposition 8, which banned same-sex marriage in California, when Ryan Kendall was 14, his parents forced him into "reparative" therapy after reading his diary and discovering he was gay. He spent about a year and a half in this conversion therapy with Dr. Joseph

Nicolosi, then-executive director of the National Association for Reparative Therapy of Homosexuality (NARTH) who claims to be able to cure people of being gay, before he eventually ran away from home.[55]

Laura Elena Calvo had worked for sixteen years in the Josephine County Sherriff's Office in Oregon, serving as a SWAT commander and a detective in the Major Crimes Unit. She was named Deputy of the Year, taught at the Oregon Police Academy, and received commendations for various accomplishments. During this time she lived as a man, her gender assigned at birth, even though she would have preferred to live as a woman. One day, another officer found some of her female clothing after a storage unit where she kept her female clothing had been burglarized. Laura Elena was sent for a psychiatric evaluation by doctors chosen by the Sheriff, declared unfit for duty, and terminated. In this case, the system was implicitly telling Calvo to conform to the acceptable gender or be fired.[56]

The second demand is to hide your true identity and pretend to be something you are not. The demand to hide/pretend operates when society requires an LGB person to take active steps to act straight. For example, if a lesbian employee feels she has to talk about a boyfriend instead of a girlfriend, she is being faced with a demand to hide/pretend. A young gay male student may be treated badly if he does not play along with his straight peers and show interest in women. The longstanding policy of the Boy Scouts upheld by the Supreme Court in 2000 prohibited "open and avowed" homosexuality, presumably permitting homosexuals who keep it hidden. As of 2014, the Boy Scouts of America will no longer ban openly gay scouts from participating in the organization. However, they will continue to bar gay adult leaders, effectively sending a message that young gay men must eliminate public expressions of homosexuality upon reaching adulthood.

Transgender people are also faced with the demand to hide their true gender identity. Throughout the 1800s and 1900s many municipalities prohibited public cross-dressing, defining it as lewd behavior, though not necessarily prohibiting cross-dressing at home. In one study, 32 percent of transgender people felt they had to present themselves as the wrong gender in order to keep their jobs. A large majority (71 percent) said they had, at some point, hidden their gender, 59 percent delayed their transition to avoid discrimination, and nearly half said they stayed in a job they wanted to leave because of fear of discrimination.[57]

National studies have found that workers feel they need to hide their sexuality at work because they fear that being open may be an obstacle to advancement (28 percent of LGBT workers), that they may be fired (17 percent of LGBT workers), or that they feared for their personal safety (40 percent of transgender workers).[58]

The last demand is to downplay the identity enough so that one can pass as straight. In this way, others don't have to deal with the presence of a homosexual or transgender person in their presence. A demand to downplay/pass is reflected in the instruction "I don't mind if you are gay. Just don't be obvious about it." Gay parents in custody cases have their kids taken away because their relationships with people of the same gender are considered "flagrant." Public disorderliness laws may be applied disproportionately, laws may punish attire that deviates from particular gender standards, and medical staff may avoid questions relevant to LGBT people. Culturally, the downplay/pass demand may be reflected in unwritten rules that workers and professionals must stick with gender stereotypes; refrain from activism and expression; stay away from the gay angle; maintain alliances with mainstream organizations, churches, music, and sports; and remain single or celibate in order to be fully accepted by colleagues or family. Downplaying and passing cuts off honest interaction with the community and interferes with the formation of support systems to survive health or financial crises.

An historic example of the demand to downplay/pass is the case of Robin Shahar, a lesbian who had accepted an offer of employment with the Attorney General of Georgia. She was out during the application process. Her new bosses knew she was gay when she was hired. After she accepted the job—but before she began work—she had a public commitment ceremony, and her offer was subsequently withdrawn by the Attorney General. She sued. At trial, the Attorney General testified that she was not fired because she was gay; she was fired because she was public about it. He did not want to employ a flaunter.[59]

Military service offers a good example of these three types of demands. Rules saying homosexuals or transgender people cannot serve in the military are demands to convert. Turn straight or go to jail. The Don't Ask Don't Tell policy was, in theory, a requirement to downplay/pass. If you are a homosexual, you do not have to take affirmative measures to hide, just remain silent. This was based on the assumption that one could serve in the military and the issue of orientation would just never come up. In reality, the truth of one's life comes up all the time when working with other people. Information about the sexual orientation of service members was used against them and many people had to hide/pretend. Now that DADT is no longer operative, people with different sexual orientations and gender identities (note that transsexuals are prohibited from serving in the military) will continue to face the demand to downplay/pass simply because of cultural pressure. Will service members be harassed if they mention their partners too much? Will they find their lives easier if they downplay and shrink their identities?

These requirements limit more than identity. They limit one's capabilities to fully engage in the activity of life. In schools across the country, LGBT teachers are told to hide or downplay their identities in ways that heterosexual teachers are not. Hiding and downplaying limits the ability of individuals to show same-sex public affection, such as when a gay couple was told by a flight attendant that they were disturbing other passengers by kissing and they would be removed from the plane. It limits the ability of LGBT people to become activists for their own cause.

The requirements to hide/pretend and downplay/pass can come from LGBT or non-LGBT people. In fact, this requirement is as much a result of a clash between LGBT people as it is between anyone else. This requirement separates out the normal gays from the queers, the dykes from the lesbians, the gender queers from transgender people the wedded couples from the alternative families, and so on. Some combination of these demands can be felt by most LGBT people.

Individual Lived Experience

Keeping the larger patterns of discrimination in mind, we can now shift our focus and try to understand the lived experience of individual LGBT people: What are the pathways to development and how do stigma and prejudice affect the needs of LGBT people to achieve higher levels of well being?

INDIVIDUAL IDENTITY DEVELOPMENT. Creating a useful yet flexible model for analyzing the development of LGBT people is an initial challenge. Theories of personality and identity development could serve as a starting point. I do not mean to dismiss or minimize the fact that, in many respects, LGBT people develop along the same lines as anyone else. However, I take up issues specific to LGBT people in order to demonstrate how we might craft an agenda that fully accounts for LGBT identities and people.

The field of lesbian and gay studies has several paradigms for articulating how lesbians, gay men, and bisexuals develop a sexual orientation and identity. The field of gender and transgender studies has very few paradigms for the development of gender-nonconforming identities, and none of them seem satisfactory. More development in both areas is necessary. At a minimum, many views of human development support the premise that orientation and gender identities are real. Some views hold that these identities are innate—based in biology or very early life experiences, fixed throughout a person's life span, and beyond the reasonable ability of the individual to manipulate. Others say that nurture, environment, and social norms create sexual orientation and gender identities. A middle road interpretation holds that sexual orientation and gender identity are a core part of a person and that ways these identities are thought of and expressed involve elements of choice. The outward expression and the inward interpretation a person has about their orientation and identity are heavily predicated on the social and cultural environment.

We can see the differences in the ways people see themselves by the ways they label their orientation and identity. In one study, 19 female-to-male transgender people used 33 combinations of labels to describe themselves. The terms gay, lesbian, and bisexual are equally as fluid.[60]

Several psychologists have developed models of homosexuality, many of them imperfectly referred to as "stage" models. The name seems to indicate that one goes through stages, one after the other, until one reaches the pinnacle of perfect gayness. Most stage models actually identify separate areas of development that individuals go through and revisit throughout their lives depending on what issues are most pressing. Nevertheless, these stage models resonate with many LGBT people because they reflect their own experiences with periods of wondering, internal conflict, and acceptance. Almost all of them include the milestone of coming out.

Australian psychologist Vivienne Cass developed a model that focuses on the development of same-sex orientation over time in one's life, rather than on the outcomes reached at a single point in time. Cass identifies six stages of self-perception and behavior: [61]

1. Identity Questioning: "What are these thoughts, feelings and attractions? Could I be gay?" The response could be positive or negative judgments, acceptance, denial, and/or rejection, inhibited behavior, exploration and testing of relationships, career and social identity, or seeking or avoiding information about individual development.

2. Identity Comparison: "Maybe this does apply to me." Accepting the possibility of being gay or lesbian, the individual examines wider and longer term implications in the relevant context, focuses concern on loss of previous expectations of heterosexual life, makes a distinction between private thoughts and public behavior, and seeks out community and resources.

3. Identity Tolerance: "I am not alone." The individual acquires a language to talk about the identity, recognizes sets of options open to him or herself as a gay or lesbian individual, and solidifies beliefs about differences between him or herself and heterosexuals. At this stage the

individual can benefit from information and exploration of feelings about identities (heterosexism, internalized homophobia). Positive contacts with other lesbian and gay people will contribute to positive sense of self; negative contact will hamper development.

4. Identity Acceptance: "I will be okay." The task at this stage is to deal with inner tension of no longer subscribing to society's norms, attempting to bring congruence between private (positive) views of self and public (negative) views of self. The individual makes choices about coming-out, fitting in, disclosing, and being associated with different segments of society.

5. Identity Pride: The individual establishes views of non-homosexual people and deals with anger, pride and incongruent treatment. He or she focuses on gay people as sources of support, friendship, career, and business connections.

6. Identity Synthesis: The person integrates his or her sexual identity with all other aspects of self, and sexual orientation becomes only one aspect of self rather than the entire identity. The task is to integrate gay and lesbian identity so that instead of being THE identity, it is an aspect of self. Possible responses can be to continue feeling anger toward heterosexism, but with decreased intensity, or to allow trust of others to increase and build. Gay and lesbian identity is integrated with all aspects of "self".

Gender identity operates at multiple levels in an individual's development. In all societies, there are sets of characteristics that are attributed to males or females. Which set of characteristics are identified with which gender varies greatly from person to person. Gender identity includes one's private sense of gender and one's biology, as well as one's conduct and expression.

The World Professional Association of Transgender Health (WPATH) notes that a generation of transsexual, transgender, and gender-nonconforming individuals has produced evidence about the diversity of the development of gender identity. Some perceive their identity as transitioning from one gender to another. Some identify themselves as conforming to a traditional male or female role (i.e., as a member of the other sex). Others affirm an identity that transcends the binary male/female concept of gender. WPATH notes that normal epidemiological studies on the prevalence of transsexualism have not been conducted, reflecting the general need for further development of an evidence basis to evaluate approaches to improve the well being of transgender people.[62]

Canadian sociologist Aaron Devor proposed a stage theory to gender identity formation. This theory has fourteen stages and explores comparisons with one's birth sex followed by identity comparisons with different sexes. (1) Abiding Anxiety, (2) Identity Confusion About Originally Assigned Gender and Sex, (3) Identity Comparisons About Originally Assigned Gender and Sex, (4) Discovery

of Transsexualism, (5) Identity Confusion about Transsexualism, (6) Identity Comparisons about Transsexualism, (7) Tolerance of Transsexual Identity, (8) Delay
Before Acceptance of Transsexual Identity, (9) Acceptance of Transsexualism Identity, (10) Delay Before
Transition, (11) Transition, (12) Acceptance of Post-
transition Gender and Sex Identities, (13) Integration, and
(14) Pride.

Incorporated in Devor's theory are concepts that underlie all identity formation. These are witnessing and
mirroring. Witnessing is the desire that we have to be
witnessed by others in order to be who we believe ourselves to be. Mirroring involves identifying with some-
body else who is, in our belief, similar to ourselves and
who is, in our belief, a person with an insider perspective
on the group with which we identify. Both of these things
are social processes that require the capability to interact
and relate to others.[63]

These theories seem to all have some common messages about what LGBT people need for development,
including the importance of being able to make choices,
to have knowledge about others who may have similar
identities, to be able to envision a life-path which incorporates an authentic identity, to be able to live in a community and establish supportive relationships and
networks, and to express one's self honestly and without
fear. These capabilities can serve as the basis for a national agenda. LGBT groups can examine their own programs

to evaluate whether they actually increase the capabilities of individuals in this way. An essential part of the formation of such an agenda would be to understand the realities of LGBT people.

BARRIERS TO FULL DEVELOPMENT. Every person will face some level of life's challenges – death, conflict, prejudice, violence, rejection – which can produce various levels of annoyance or debilitating stress. Marginalized people can face an additional set of stressors as a result of the stigma and repeated discrimination they face. For LGB people, this "minority stress," as it is called, requires special adaptive and coping mechanisms not required by heterosexual, gender conforming people.[64] There is currently much less research on transgender people, so I limit this discussion to LGB people, but the possible presence of minority stress in the lives of transgender people seems evident.

Minority stress can affect the lives of LGB people in four different ways, each of which is referred to as a "minority stress process." First, chronic and acute prejudice events and conditions can trigger a stress process. Prejudice events include rejection by family members, harassment at work, assault and derision by community members, or other events symbolizing the deep cultural meaning of worthlessness assigned to LGBT people.

Second, a stress process can be caused by the expectation of such events and conditions, as well as the vigilance required by such expectation. This dynamic is subtle for those who do not experience it. For those who do, the dynamic is a familiar feeling of having to keep one's guard up against what may happen next. Members of minority groups may begin to develop expectations of discrimination after being repeatedly exposed to stigma. This constant vigilance may cause anxiety even around people who do not hold negative stereotypes.[65] A 2007 study of LGBT employees found that those who most feared that they would be discriminated against if they came out in the workplace had more physical stress-related symptoms than those who were less fearful.[66]

Third, a stress process can be caused by having to conceal or hide one's sexual orientation. Identity concealment can be a protective mechanism to avoid a more acute prejudice event. Nevertheless, it alters decisions, mood, and interactions in a way that is not experienced by those who do not have to conceal or hide themselves. First, it takes significant psychological resources to conceal identity. Individuals may develop a preoccupation with the prospect of being discovered. Second, the individual is denied the psychological and health benefits that come from honest expression and sharing of emotions and experiences with others. Third, LGB people are cut off from the ability to develop social support and coping networks. The role of social support networks in increasing health and well-being has been very well documented. The formation of these networks is limited by stigma.[67]

Last, stress can be caused by the internalization of social stigma. All people, LGB and straight people, can develop and propagate negative stereotypes about gay people. Such stereotypes, when acquired by LGB people, can limit one's sense of aspirations, motivations, and capacity for intimacy. An LGB person must, during the realization of being LGB, be able to chart a new life course which incorporates sexual identity. Internalized stigma is a barrier to development of this possible self.[68]

These four processes can produce serious health consequences. Distress, anxiety, depression and low self-esteem are possible outcomes. Anxiety is a predictor of substance use disorders as the individual attempts to relieve tension and fear. Researchers have found that gay youth who experience rejection from those to whom they disclose their sexual identity have higher rates of subsequent alcohol, cigarette, and marijuana use.[69] Overall, researchers have found a connection between stigma and prejudice and health outcomes for LGB populations in the United States.[70]

Marginalization because of sexual orientation and gender identity is also intertwined with poverty and financial injustice. I mention both poverty and financial injustice because they are two separate issues, each deserving a response. When Edie Windsor's wife, Thea Spyer, died, the federal government refused to recognize their marriage because of the so-called Defense of Marriage Act. Spyer left her estate to Windsor. The inheritance would have been tax-free if the marriage were recognized. Because of the federal law blocking recognition, Windsor was required to pay $360,000 in taxes. Windsor sued the federal government and eventually won a dramatic victory at the U.S. Supreme Court.

Edie Windsor suffered a financial injustice. Her story was clear, compelling, and unfair. As a plaintiff she was loving and sympathetic. However, this was not a narrative of poverty. Windsor was well-educated and had a successful career with IBM. Spyer was a psychologist and had a practice in Manhattan. They vacationed in the Hamptons, travelled to Canada to marry, and acquired property and investments over the forty-plus years of their relationship. The financial injustice that she experienced was made even more vivid by the backdrop of the years that they spent together, building a life together and prospering within a long-term, loving relationship.

There is a pattern for many of the relationship recognition cases bought by equality advocates: A couple lived life on a generally successful trajectory, only to have that life yanked away by a singular act of non-recognition, often leaving one partner in a relatively poor position. Good financial injustice stories often start with good finances: well employed gay men being denied foster parent status; partners with good health insurance being denied coverage; wealthy lesbians being denied an athletic club membership. These are all compelling stories of injustice that have made the clear point that same-sex couples are treated differently.

The narrative of poverty is different. Poverty can be defined in a variety of ways. Some definitions are based on the income of an individual or a household. The federal government defines the Federal Poverty Line as an income threshold which takes into account the size of the household, the number of children under 18, and the age of the householder. This definition, while simple, often does not tell the full story. Other definitions of poverty attempt to account for its multi-dimensional nature. Poverty is a deprivation across a number of areas such as food, clothing, housing, healthcare, safety, education, and decent work. These different definitions are not in conflict; they simply explain different levels of complexity of the same dynamic.

For LGBT people, poverty can act as a limitation on sexuality and gender expression, forcing people into lives they do not choose. Conversely, LGBT people may face limitations on their opportunities and wealth which can result in poverty. The Institute for Development Studies, an internationally known think tank in the United Kingdom, has theorized several ways in which poverty impacts people of different sexual orientation and gender identity:

> *Lack of information:* Poverty can restrict education and information about sexuality, health, legal rights, or even information about other LGBT people and role models. Lower levels of

knowledge can lead to bullying, depression, and increased transmission of sexually transmitted infections.

Places of the poor: Poorer locations often have fewer health and social services, less police protection, and more violence. Individuals who bear more stigmas, such as transgender people, are often restricted to living in poorer areas.

Lack of support networks: Those who do not conform to sexual norms have a higher chance of being excluded from religious organizations, clubs, and social networks that are often the source of support during crises.

Lack of political clout: Marginalization of gender non-conformity hinders efforts to use the political process to respond to needs. It is hard to get involved in politics or form organizations that are taken seriously by the dominant political groups.

Limited relationship options: Poorer people simply may not have as many options for forming new relationships. They may not have access to the same groups and places where one can meet others who are seek similar things and are supportive.

Expense of obtaining equality: Seeking to adopt a child or make a claim in court may require an attorney. Even being a witness to a hate crime case may require taking time off of work. These kinds of expenses may not be possible for a wage worker.[71]

Many LGBT people are poor. The stereotype of well-to-do gay men in *Modern Family* and *Will and Grace* has become an attractive image of the gay community, but poverty among LGBT people should be no surprise. In many cases, limitations on LGBT peoples' earning ability, health, and education start early. The story of Seth, a client of the American Civil Liberties Union (ACLU), is heartbreakingly common. In fifth grade, students started calling him "gay." As he got older, the verbal abuse and taunts were more frequent and severe. By seventh grade, other students constantly called him "queer" and "fag." He was afraid to use the restroom or be in the boys' locker room before gym class. One student reported that a teacher called Seth "fruity" in front of an entire class. Seth's mother told the ACLU that her pleas for help to the school were often brushed aside. Seth's grades eventually dropped from A's and B's to failing as the harassment continued. School became so intolerable that Seth hung himself from a tree in his backyard.[72]

Research suggests that a disproportionate number of homeless youth are LGBT. An estimated 1.6 million youth in the U.S. experience homelessness each year; and research suggests that between 20 and 40 percent of them identify as LGBT.[73]

Recent studies from the Gay, Lesbian and Straight Education Network (GLSEN) and in the *Journal of Adoles-*

cent Health tell us that 30 percent of LGB students reported missing one day of class in the past month because of safety concerns, compared to 8 percent of a national sample of secondary students.[74] Another analysis shows that in the Midwestern United States, LGBT people are less likely to have completed a college degree by age 25 than non-LGBT people.[75] Poor experiences in school can have long-term effects. According to a recent report on transgender discrimination, transgender people who were harassed and abused by teachers showed dramatically worse health outcomes than others.[76] Research by the Williams Institute based on data about people in same-sex couples shows that low levels of education are particularly harmful for the financial prospects of people in same-sex couples. Looking at people without a high school diploma, those in a different-sex married couple have a poverty rate of 19 percent. Men without a diploma in same-sex couples have a poverty rate of 20 percent. Women without a diploma in same-sex couples have a poverty rate of 33 percent.[77]

The link between stigma and financial outcomes makes common sense. Employers are subject to the same prejudices as other people, and exclusion from workplace opportunities can limit opportunities for income. In a nationally representative survey of LGB adults in 2013, one in five people reported having been treated unfairly by an employer as a result of their sexual orientation or gender identity.[78] Of people who were open about their sexual orientation at work, harassment was the most common form of discrimination reported. However, one-third of LGB people were not open about being LGB in the workplace. Only 5.8 percent of bisexuals were generally open about their sexual orientation.[79] Though these studies involve self-reporting, evidence from controlled experiments indicates that bias operates in the workplace. In these experiments, researchers create scenarios which permit comparison of the treatment of LGB workers to the treatment of non-LGB workers. For example, one method used by researchers is to send out pairs of resumes in response to vacancy announcements posted by employers seeking job applicants. The pairs are similar in all respects, except that one resume includes some indication that the applicant is LGB. The researchers then measure the response by employers to the resumes. In a review of nine such controlled experiments, eight of the studies revealed discriminatory bias.[80]

Among transgender people, the rate of those who say they have experienced harassment or mistreatment at work, or have taken actions to avoid it, climbs to nine in ten people. Forty-seven percent of trans people report having been fired, passed up for promotion, or not hired because of their gender identity.

Difficulties in the workplace can produce financial difficulties. A 2014 report sponsored by the U.S. Department of Health and Human Services found evidence in nationally representative, population-based surveys, that suggests that LGBT people are more likely to face economic difficulties than are non-LGBT people.[81] Professor M.V. Lee Badgett, a Professor at the University of Massachusetts, Amherst, as well as a Senior Scholar at UCLA's Williams Institute, has pioneered the field in looking at the relationship between sexual orientation and poverty. She and others have analyzed data from the U.S. Census Bureau and other data sources to compare the rates of poverty among LGB people to the rates of poverty for heterosexual people.[82] In general, same-sex couples are more vulnerable to poverty than different-sex married couples. Poverty rates for female same-sex couples are higher than those of married different-sex couples. Male couples are more likely to be poor than married different-sex couples after controlling for other characteristics that influence poverty. African-Americans in same-sex couples have poverty rates at least twice the rates of different-sex married African-Americans. African-American men in same-sex couples are more than six times as likely to be poor than White men in same-sex couples, and African-American women with female partners are three times more likely to be poor than White women with female partners.

Children of LGB parents are especially vulnerable to poverty. Children in same-sex couple households are almost twice as likely to be poor as children in married different-sex households. African-American children in gay male households have the highest poverty rate (52 percent) of children in any household type (same- or oppo-site-sex, male or female). The poverty gap is highest for children aged 0-5 who live with same-sex couples.

The level of poverty among transgender people is acute. The National Transgender Discrimination Survey looked at 6,400 transgender and gender non-conforming participants from all 50 states. Ninety percent of transgender people responding to a national survey on transgender discrimination said they had experienced workplace mistreatment. Nearly half said that they had been passed up for a job or a promotion due to their gender identity, and about a quarter reported that they lost a job.[83] Transgender people were four times more likely to have a household income of less than $10,000 per year compared to the general population. Transgender people of color had an unemployment rate four times the national average, and almost one in five reported being homeless at least one time in their life.[84]

LGBT people of color face compounded marginaliza-tion. According to a Williams Institute analysis of Census 2000 data, almost one in five members of same-sex cou-ples in the United States are people of color, and one in eight are Latino/Latina. Like people of color generally, LGBT people of color are more likely to live in poverty. For example, African-American same-sex couples are sig-nificantly more likely to be poor than their African-American married heterosexual counterparts and are roughly three times more likely to live in poverty than white same-sex couples.[85] Transgender people of color fared worse than other transgender people in areas of income, health, homelessness, and abuse by police.[86]

The effects of exclusion can accumulate throughout one's life and manifest themselves in the lived experiences of older LGBT Americans. According to a report funded by the National Institutes of Health and the National Institute on Aging, the number of LGBT older adults in the U.S. will double to more than three million by 2030. Older LGBT people face isolation and exclusion from support services available to other seniors. Within a few years, half of all people with HIV will be age 50 or over.[87] Researchers at the University of Washington School of Social Work in Seattle found in the first nationwide LGBT study on aging and health that LGBT seniors experience higher rates of disability and physical and mental anguish, as well as lack of access to services compared to the non-LGBT population in the United States.[88]

The primary sources of retirement income for most Americans all can be influenced by stigma earlier in life. Social security payments are based on salary levels earlier in life. Because of the demise of defined benefit plans, retirement income from retirement plans is determined by how much individuals were able to contribute during their lifetime. Lastly, income from interest, dividends, and rentals depends on the level of assets previously acquired. Poor people have fewer such assets. Female same-sex couples were found to have almost twenty percent less income in retirement than married different-sex couples. On average, female same-sex couples depended more on Social Security benefits and received fifteen percent less in Social Security benefits.[89]

Contrary to the myth of affluence of gay people is the fact that some LGBT populations receive government benefits for low-income people at a significantly higher rate than non-LGBT populations. For instance, in one analysis, same-sex couples are more likely to receive cash assistance and Supplemental Nutrition Assistance Program (SNAP) benefits than similar married different-sex couples. In another analysis, bisexual women ages 18 – 44 were more likely than heterosexual women to report receiving cash assistance and SNAP benefits. These higher participation rates may be due to LGB people not encountering difficulties receiving benefits. Though, there is no research that either supports or refutes this belief, differences in laws and legal burdens on same-sex households may also be a reason.[90]

These data tell part of the story. One component of the approach I am suggesting includes a strong emphasis on research and investigation in order to complete the story. Any set of priorities in the LGBT movement must be based on an authentic understanding of the lived experience of LGBT people.

— 4 —

The Capability Approach

LGBT people need a movement that will advocate for each person to seek a life of their choosing. The quest for a better life is not only part of the human condition; it is also part of the American notion of liberty and justice. Writing for the U.S. Supreme Court in the case that decriminalized sodomy, Justice Anthony Kennedy explained that the ability of a gay or lesbian person to make choices about his or her own life was at the core of American liberty:

> These matters, involving the most intimate and personal choices a person may make in a lifetime, choices central to personal dignity and autonomy, are central to the liberty protected by the Fourteenth Amendment. At the heart of liberty is the right to define one's own concept of exist-

ence, of meaning, of the universe, and of the mystery of human life. Beliefs about these matters could not define the attributes of personhood were they formed under the compulsion of the State.[91]

Translating Justice Kennedy's vision into a coherent plan of action for the LGBT movement is a bit tricky. To implement this vision, I suggest that we look to the field of international human development, where these questions have been the subject of research and programming for decades. In this chapter, I trace the evolution of human development frameworks over the past several decades. The current framework, called the capabilities approach, seeks to enlarge each person's freedoms, opportunities, and well-being. I review how the capabilities approach can be used to identify components of a better life for LGBT people. I suggest a list of capabilities that each person must have in order to live a full, dignified life. This list of capabilities can be used to formulate programs and priorities for an LGBT movement which respond to the lived experiences of LGBT people.

The Evolving Meanings
of Human Development

In a biological sense, human development is the process of becoming biologically mature. In the economic sense, it has been equated to the standard of living measured by income and consumption. The concept has evolved to its current meaning, which encompasses the journey over one's life of enlarging one's freedoms, opportunities, and well-being. This journey begins before we are even born. Family background, class, and place of birth are often the most important determinants of one's life trajectory. Over the course of a life, an individual may benefit from opportunities such as a good education, supportive families and government institutions, access to quality healthcare, and a safe and encouraging environment. At the same time, we may face job loss, bad health, exclusion, and violence. Some of us may have more resilience and social capital to move in and out of these experiences with relatively little backsliding, aiming toward the better life we want to lead. Human development is about how all of these factors and experiences alter our ability to choose the life we value.

For several decades, economists used economic indicators to gauge the well-being of people internationally and locally. Traditionally, economists would look at the Gross Domestic Product (GDP) of a country to determine the standard of living. GDP is the total value of goods and services produced within a country. Per capita GDP calculates the average value of goods and services produced by each person. GDP can rise even as household income falls. GDP is an attractive measurement because it is used in nearly every country in the world, as well as every state, city, and county in the United States. The monthly and quarterly reporting of GDP statistics in the United States influences economics around the globe. The consistency of methods permits analysis of apples to apples data across borders and time periods. GDP is a very rough proxy for changes in standard of living, as increases in one are usually tied to increases in another. Yet, GDP tells us very little about how individuals are faring within an economy.

Looking at the statistics for the U.S. in 2009 and 2010, GDP was on the rise. Many economic indicators such as rising wholesale inventories, commodity prices, and construction contradicted the reality that Americans were spending more on housing and the rate of foreclosure was at record highs. It was not until 2011 and 2012 that we began to see indications of the economic status of Americans. Indeed, the theme of the Occupy protest movement and even some Tea Party activists was that general economic indicators do not reflect the daily experiences of most Americans. Statistics about national economic production are more relevant to employers than to employees, to people who owned businesses rather than people who bought from them. Setting aside instances of outright financial fraud and fiction highlighted by the Enron corruption scandal and JP Morgan's reporting failures, economic statistics have lost credibility as real measurements of individual well-being.

In the late 1980s, the United Nations formulated a "people-centered" approach to measuring human development and well-being. This approach was born out of the frustration that global economic indicators did not fully tell the story of the health of children, literacy rates, household prosperity, and other factors vital to the well-being of individuals. Human development became defined as the process of enlarging people's opportunities and improving their well-being. This put individuals at the center of the equation, and it recognized that money and economic growth were a means to an end. Rather than seeing human beings as inputs to economic growth, the value of money was measured in its ability to increase health, promote education, and so on. Following this equation, discussion of human development would require looking at the length of one's life, the level of one's knowledge, and the roles of people in families and communities, and seeing if nations made progress over time.

The United Nations issued the first Human Development Report in 1990.[92] Every year since, the United Nations has commissioned a team of scholars and practitioners to independently draft an annual report that studies the conditions affecting human development globally. Governments, international financial institutions, and advocacy organizations use these encyclopedia-length reports to identify problems and craft policies and programs. Each report examines conditions generally. Additionally, each report focuses on a few "dimensions" of human development. Examples of dimensions include health, human rights, the environment, food, parenting, creativity and productivity, being part of a community, the ability to migrate, and access to information.[93]

Data for this report is gathered through multiple studies all over the globe. The Demographic and Health Survey is a standardized survey conducted by governments and non-governmental organizations in all countries receiving international aid. Trained data gatherers use a variety of data collection methods including household visits, interviews in social service agencies, and data collection through government programs. Data include information about health, family, income, violence, diet, consumer patterns, education, and so on.

These reports are often accompanied by numerical indices, the best known of which is the Human Development Index (HDI).[94] Countries are ranked according to how their population scores on the HDI. One of the primary reasons for the creation of such an index was its ability to communicate, through a single number, the level of human development. While reducing such a complex matter to a single data point does little to help refine discussion, economists recognized that expecting policymakers and the public to sort through reams of data was not feasible. They were right. The Human Development Index is how many people are introduced to this issue.

Those who work in this area full-time spend less time on the index itself than they do on the volumes of data that underlie the HDI. Statistically, the HDI is a composite score based on measurements of education, life expectancy, and income (actually gross national income at purchasing power parity per capita, but most just refer to this as the "income" score). Leading a long healthy life, maintaining a decent material standard of living, and access to knowledge are three core capabilities that are universally valued around the world. Health, employment, and education are also firmly held concerns for the LGBT movement, along with access to health services for transgender people, provision of services to people with HIV/AIDS, employment non-discrimination protections, safe schools, and comprehensive sexuality education.

The wealth of data collected to create the HDI can also be used to answer many other questions. For instance, the HDI does not tell us about inequalities within a country. In 2010, the UNDP introduced the Inequality-adjusted Human Development Index (IHDI) to measure the average level of human development for people in a country once inequality in the distribution of health, education, and income is taken into account. As a result, all countries scored less in the IHDI than the HDI due to inequality. The U.S. ranks fourth in the world on the

HDI, but it falls by 19 spots to rank 23rd globally on the IHDI.[95]

The Gender Inequality Index looks at reproductive health, women's empowerment, and labor market participation. The U.S. ranks 47th internationally, which is exceptionally low for a country whose HDI and even IHDI rank much higher.[96] The United Nations Development Programme (UNDP) and the World Bank have developed indicators and analysis of violence, education, carbon output, health, and a wide variety of other dimensions. This data is accessible to the public and is used by public and private companies to determine priorities for each country.

The Capabilities Approach

The basis of the current human development framework used by the international development community is called the "capabilities approach," developed initially by Harvard economist Amartya Sen.[97] Under this approach, the goal of development is to enlarge people's capabilities. Capabilities are defined as real opportunities to engage in activities that people want to engage in such as working, being part of a community, having health, resting, having knowledge. The concept of opportunity is central to the definition of a capability. Capabilities are what people could do, even if they do not chose to do so. Functionings are what people actually do. Thus, an individual's capabilities includes what they actually do, their functionings, as well as their opportunities to do other things, their capabilities.

Consider the example of two women who work every waking hour and engage in very little leisure or social activities. In each case, heavy work hours and low leisure time is that person's functioning. The key to understanding their well-being is to know whether they have other options, or capabilities. Perhaps one of the women has chosen to work long hours because she finds it fulfilling, she may be rewarded for extra-long hours, and she willingly foregoes leisure time and social activities. The other woman has no choice but to work long hours in order to make a subsistence living, and she has no other options for making a living. Even though the two women have the same functionings, the first woman has more capabilities. Thus, according to the capability approach, the first woman is better off.

Someone who has not eaten a meal today may not have the capability to eat, which means they are starving. Or that person may have the capability to eat, but instead they choose to fast. Functionally, both people are not taking in food, but they have different capabilities and therefore are at different levels of development.

Someone with a high level of capabilities has the freedom to choose the "better life" they want to live. Someone with a lower level of capabilities has fewer choices. Their choices may be restricted by economics, stigma, the actions of others in society, the government, the environment, their own bodies, or their families. The capabilities approach values policies according to their impact on people's capabilities rather than their impact on functionings.

The LGBT movement shares three concerns with the capabilities approach. First is the recognition that each person, just by being human, is of equal dignity and worth. At first, this principle seems easy enough to accept. However, let's look at other principles of community development. Some leaders and nations might say that programs should be chosen according to what provides the greatest good for the greatest number of people. If sacrificing the well-being of twenty percent of the population results in an even larger increase in the well-being of the other eighty percent, is that preferable? How far up or down the utility curve are we willing to go? And who sets the utility curve? Men, women, white people? At some point, the "greatest good" argument supports the notion that the lives of twenty percent of the people can be "utilized" for the purpose of the lives of the eighty percent.

The notion that each person has equal worth, if we fully accept it, limits how much we can accept the utility approach. In the United States, the courts have played the role of protector of stigmatized minorities. One person's right to express an idea outweighs the fact that everyone else disagrees with him. One person's potential innocence outweighs the fact that everyone else might be better off if that person were jailed. These limitations require unpopular and tough decisions, but they are a hallmark of the governance to which we aspire.

Second, this approach assumes that the worth of a person includes the power to make moral choices for themselves, including the ability to plan a life in accordance with one's own values. The ability to define and make moral choices is a centerpiece of the LGBT agenda.

Third, this approach recognizes that people are diverse. Not everyone is the same. From at least a purely economic level, people differ in their ability to use money, food, and other goods for their own well-being. And they differ in what they consider to be well-being in the first place. Simply put, a well-developed person is one who has the capability to function well, however he or she defines that, with the goods and services at their disposal. This recognition that different people have different desires and face different contexts is what makes this approach powerful for LGBT people.

Defining a Better Life

Given limited resources, what capabilities should leaders prioritize? The capability to give birth to a child might be important for some people and irrelevant for others who might not want to be parents. Some might value the capability to express, through the choice of dress and appearance, one's gender differently from the sex assigned at birth. Again, this is not helpful for everyone. Some people might want the capacity to remain a sexually active single person or to conduct one's life as a Spanish speaker and not be shut out of community activities.

Because different people value different things there is no universal "list" of capabilities. One of the aspects of the capabilities approach is that each person has the freedom to decide how to live. Amartya Sen argues that endorsing a particular list of capabilities is the same thing as predetermining what freedoms people should value. Indeed, he recognizes the fact that some people in some cultures might choose lives that are inconsistent with modern human rights standards.[98] His deference to community-based priorities is commendable. He honors diversity in a deep and disciplined way. However, insofar as Sen would give permission to communities to develop their own list of capabilities, I enthusiastically take the opportunity to develop a list of capabilities from my perspective. As a gay man who has worked in the LGBT community for decades, I feel comfortable proposing a list for the purpose of beginning a community-based conversation to produce priorities for the American LGBT community.

As an advocacy movement, the LGBT community should stake a claim rooted in human rights. The movement should adopt an agenda that stakes a claim on a society that responds to all people while insuring a space for LGBT people. Without attempting to make claims about all sexual orientations and gender identities everywhere, the current American LGBT communities have enough knowledge about the lives of LGBT people to propose specific measures to increase well-being and development.

Martha Nussbaum, a political philosopher who worked with Amartya Sen on the development of the human development index, encourages us to identify a set of capabilities that are broad enough to be universally useful, yet specific enough to give us guidance about the aims of government and society.[99] Nussbaum's starting point seems to be the same inquiry made by the ancients about what made up a good life. She creates a list of ten capabilities. This includes capabilities that are so central that removal of one of them makes a life that is not worthy of human beings. Because of this, one could not trade a loss of one capability for a gain in another. Her list also reflects basic human rights.

Thus, my starting point is Nussbaum's list, which I adopt with some modifications. This list is assembled based on considerations of four factors: 1) the realities of LGBT people, 2) a commitment to pluralism, 3) a requirement of dignity, and 4) public salience.

Foremost, the movement must advocate for a set of capabilities that responds to the realities of LGBT people. The agenda must be grounded in a deep understanding of identity development and human development from LGBT perspectives. All people need to be able to advance through the course of one's life, progressing from infancy into adolescence then adulthood and old-age. A life-course perspective of human development identifies socially defined norms of expected life transitions as major benchmarks of well-being. Such a perspective recognizes that individuals need different types of support in order to be successful at different life stages. Such a perspective also recognizes that limits on development during one state in life can increase vulnerabilities later in life. For instance, the experience of bullying in school may result in decreased academic performance and increased poverty later in life. Thus, the first capability listed is the ability to progress through life's stages.

Sexual orientation and gender identity may not develop along a linear path. Vivienne Cass's and Aaron Devor's theories about the development of sexual orientation and gender identity (set out above) indicate that in order to maximize the potential for full development, LGBT people need to cycle through a series of stages in the life and must at all times have enough information and education to understand one's self, positive contacts with other people and engage with a community, permission and support to explore feelings, and the ability to express one's self. Accordingly, the list includes the capabilities to learn, reason, form thoughts, beliefs, and perceptions, and experience emotional and mental states.

Second, the list must reflect a commitment to a pluralistic society—freedom of speech and expression, freedom to associate with others, and opportunity to participate in governance. The right to express one's self has been a cornerstone of the LGBT movement. The very first gay rights case in the U.S. Supreme Court was about freedom of speech, when the U.S. Postal Service attempted to ban materials dealing with homosexuality.[100] The very first case brought by the Lambda Legal Defense and Education Fund was about the freedom of LGBT groups to form and register as organizations.[101] Anti-violence projects are establishing safety for those in the community whose ability to express themselves is endangered by threats. Indeed, many parts of the movement are premised on the assumption that coming out is the key to equality.

The capability to affiliate is a particularly strong component of the LGBT movement's contribution to a pluralistic society, though one often not placed within an "advocacy" framework. Every year, millions of LGBT people in the U.S. participate in pride events. Some use these events as a platform for advocacy, and others as a place to individually express themselves in ways that are unavailable in other parts of their lives. Others see pride events as opportunities for commerce and livelihood (though some think the commercialization of pride is a terrible thing, these vendors and workers are doing something we generally want people to do—make a living—and usually at modest levels). Black Prides and Dyke Marches have grown in number and accessibility.

A glance at the calendar of any LGBT community center will show meeting rooms filled each day with LGBT people associating in ways they feel add value to their lives. LGBT sports leagues and athletic clubs serve as a good visible example of structured associations that take place in the U.S. LGBT community. Tens of thousands of LGBT people participate in LGBT athletic clubs. Tom Waddell, founder of the Gay Games, said, "We need to discover more about the process of our sexual liberation and apply it meaningfully to other forms of liberation." Waddell writes:

> The Gay Games are not separatist, they are not exclusive, they are not oriented to victory, and they are not for commercial gain. They are, however, intended to bring a global community together in friendship, to experience participation, to elevate consciousness and self-esteem, and to achieve a form of cultural and intellectual synergy.... We are involved in the process of altering opinions whose foundations lie in ignorance. We

have the opportunity to take the initiative on critical issues that affect the quality of life and we
can serve in a way that makes all people the ben-
eficiary.[102]

The Gay Games and the Out Games continue to be
among the largest global events in the LGBT community.

The highly structured personal associations of the
iconic Michigan Women's Music Festival continue to
draw enormous numbers and spawn similar events
around the country. The equally iconic and structured
International Mr. Leather contest in Chicago each year
now registers nearly 20,000 people, and its contestants
have competed in 200 local community pageants, each
raising money for local community organizations. The
2012 National Conference of Gay and Lesbian Association of Choruses had over 6,100 attendees, which is un-
doubtedly only a fraction of the people who regularly
gather with their local LGBT chorus. Thousands attend
LGBT film festivals each year. For an uncountable number of people in recovery, AA meetings held at LGBT-
friendly venues are a lifeline. PFLAG chapters and youth
support chapters can be found in each region of the
country.

Thus, the list of capabilities includes the capability to
engage in a variety of levels of affiliations, from simply
showing concern for others to engaging in community
activities to forming permanent family relationships. Pluralism also requires the capacity to engage in governance.

In part, this concerns whether a group is able to participate in governance as political leaders themselves. The evidence that legislatures are more responsive to LGBT issues if they include LGBT members is fairly clear. Pluralism also values the ability of people to engage with governance at a variety of levels. Do members of the community have the resources needed to travel to, or interact with, to government offices? Do they have the information needed to know how to speak for themselves and to whom? The capabilities approach values not just obtaining a good set of rules about who can participate in government; rather, it values the opportunity of individuals to participate. Put another way, the capability of pluralism is not checking all the doors to government to see if they are open; it is checking all the people to make sure they can get in if they want to. Justice is not determined by the state of the institution. It is established by the capacity of individuals. Thus, the list includes the capacity to participate in governance and political decisions that affect one's life.

Pluralism is also about the capacity of LGBT people to participate in governance with those who do not support them. As psychologist George Weinberg says of the non-supportive, some may not know gay people (the ignorant), some may have an analysis about why they don't like gay people (the anti-gay), and some may simply be freaked out and hysterical about gay people (the homophobic).[103] Pluralism includes supporting the capacity of everyone, including the ignorant, anti-gay, and homophobic, to participate in and engage in governance.

Pluralism in a true democracy can have its troubling moments, as majoritarian views can result in ostracism of the minority. What keeps an unsupportive population from going to the government and persuading everyone to cut off all the other capacities of LGBT people? Or, to keep LGBT people well-fed and well-educated, but locked in a room somewhere (which some call the closet)? These concerns lead us to the third feature of the capabilities list.

Thirdly, the list must adhere to the requirement of dignity. Nussbaum's concept of dignity is different from the concept that many of us associate with the word. Unlike most other constitutions, the Constitution of the United States does not have a dignity clause. Dignity clauses have been the basis for decriminalizing sodomy under the Constitution of Montana, legalizing same-sex marriage in Canada, assuring equal immigration rights for same-sex people in South Africa, and achieving the right to healthcare for LGBT people in Portugal. In these cases, dignity is a level of care that a government must exercise toward its citizens.

Nussbaum refocuses the issue of dignity by looking at the person. Dignity is the ability of a person to live life as part of society. The government's role is to protect and provide infrastructures and institutions for individuals to live well, in the company of others, while engaging with others. Dignity is revealed not just by being accompanied by others in life but by sharing ourselves with others.

This approach to dignity closely tracks the needs of LGBT people to live in a culture that supports social connection and inclusion. The stage theory of gender identity development recognizes the universality of a requirement to live in a connected, interdependent manner:

> Each of us are social beings, and as such we live in a sea of other humans with whom we interact during most of the waking hours of our lives. Even when we are not in contact with others, we devote a tremendous amount of our psychic energies to being psychologically engaged with others. It would therefore be difficult to underestimate the powerful effects that the opinions of others have on each of us.
>
> Each of us has a deep need to be witnessed by others for who we are. Each of us wants to see ourselves mirrored in others' eyes as we see ourselves. These interactive processes, witnessing and mirroring, are part of everyone's lives. When they work well, we feel validated and confirmed—our sense of self is reinforced.[104]

Nussbaum leaves the concept purposely vague so that it can be implemented and applied according to the situation and context. In all cases, government behavior that results in someone being cut out or cut off is a violation of dignity. Official disrespect and humiliation of a person is also a violation. For Nussbaum, dignities can never be traded away because they protect the basic relationship between each individual and the government. In this way, Nussbaum insures that malice of anti-LGBT people cannot be used to trump the interests of LGBT people. If the electorate wanted to approve a law allowing the government to pay someone a thousand dollars for the right to violate their dignity, Nussbaum would say this is not permissible. Colorado's Amendment 2, which sought to exclude lesbian and gay people from the protection of state and local laws, was clearly a violation of dignity and would not be permitted under this principle. Dignity might also require programs to address intergenerational poverty among black workers or the examination of the exclusion of gay men from HIV programs in the southeast U.S. Exclusion of immigrants from certain sectors of the economy or educational institutions would be violations of dignity.

The final principle reflected in the list is that each of the capabilities has public salience. Each of the capabilities on this list relates to an area of life where the government can play a significant role as a supporter and enabler of individual choices that matter to LGBT people. The capabilities are public, in that they are impacted by government actions; they are salient, in that they are part of LGBT rights debates. For example, I have included the capability to have good health, as well as the capability to work. Both health and employment (or at least employment non-discrimination) are areas where government policy can play a significant role. Additionally, these are both issues that are high priorities for the LGBT movement agenda. In contrast, Nussbaum included on her list the capability to relate to the world of animals, plants, and nature, as well as the capability to play and engage in recreational activities. These capabilities, though important globally, are not salient to the LGBT movement.

Distilling all the considerations above produces the following list of capabilities:

1. **Development from birth to old age.** Each person should have the capability to progress through each of life's stages, from youth to the end of life's span.

2. **Health.** Each person should be able to have good health, including sexual and reproductive health, adequate nourishment, and shelter.

3. **Integrity of identity and body.** Each person should be able to have security and self-determination over their identity and body, including the expressive components of it, be free from coercion and violence, and have opportunities for sexual satisfaction.

4. **Mental, Emotional and Perceptive Capacity.** Each person should be able to use the senses and form perceptions; to form attachments, love, and longing, as well as loss of and grief

for things and persons outside themselves; to experience self-doubt, self-acceptance, gratitude, and justified anger; to not have one's mental and emotional development blighted by fear or coercion.

5. **Reasoning, Learning and Decision making capacity.** Each person should have the capability to acquire information, to form judgments about the good in the world and in one's self, to think and reason in a way cultivated by an adequate education, to engage in and express political and artistic works, to engage in belief and religion of one's choosing, and to engage in the planning and development of one's own life.

6. **Affiliation.** Each person should have the capability to live for and in relation to a community, to recognize and show concern for others, to engage in social and intimate interactions, to form and maintain family, and to be able to be treated as a dignified being whose worth is equal to that of others.

7. **Work.** Each person should have the capability to engage in decent and productive work.

8. **Participation in governance:** Each person should be able to participate effectively in political choices that govern one's life and have the rights of political participation, free speech, and freedom of association.

-5-

What the Capabilities Approach Offers

The capabilities approach advances the LGBT movement in several ways. First, it confronts the gap between the law and lived experiences. Second, it promotes rights that are important to the LGBT community. This list also pays particular attention to those issues which are of concern to the LGBT movement such as expression, relationships, health, safety, and work. Third, it incorporates cultural and racial differences.

Addressing the Gap Between the Law and Lived Experience

The hard lesson of the civil rights movements of the 60s and 70s is that the elimination of legal discrimination does not result in equality. Even though the U.S. Constitution and federal statutes include broad prohibitions of discrimination based on race, African-Americans continue to face exclusion. Even after the passage of laws addressing sex-based discrimination, women continue to make 85 cents for every dollar earned by men. Given this, it seems unlikely laws requiring formal equal treatment of LGBT people will produce full, actual equality for LGBT people.

LGBT people in some other countries, such as South Africa and some European countries, have higher levels of formal equality than here in the United States. The experience of those countries may provide a glimpse of the impact of formal equality on LGBT people. Among the best known is South Africa, where the post-apartheid constitution explicitly prohibits discrimination based on sexual orientation. That provision is part of the broader equality clause. It was not a result of a groundswell of pro-LGBT sentiment amongst South Africans. Rather, it was part of a desire to eradicate apartheid with a strong, contemporary constitution that reflected global human rights principles in place in 1996. The LGBT provision resulted from some sharp negotiation in the African National Congress and was far in advance of public sentiment about LGBT people. Although South Africans have enjoyed constitutional projection and marriage equality for several years, their lives are still sharply impacted by stigma. To this day, black lesbians outside of the urban centers face "corrective rape" by their neighbors, and black gay men and women endure systematic violence and exclusion from school and work. Police don't respond. If an LGBT person seeks treatment at a rural health center, they are as likely to get a lecture about homosexuality as receive proper medical care. The reality on the ground does not mirror the superlative legal standards.

In 2011, I travelled with a group of law professors and police officers through Serbia, Montenegro, and Croatia, three countries formed after the breakup of the former Yugoslavia. The legal systems of these countries were constructed after 2005 and were designed to reflect the modern governance schemes that made up the European Union. According to data assembled by the International Lesbian and Gay Association, these countries have some of the best laws in the world for LGBT people—hate crimes laws, anti-discrimination protections, relationship recognition, health care, sets of rights that would be considered gigantic steps forward if they were to be obtained nationally, here, in the United States. I wanted to see what such a system looked like.

I arrived in Belgrade, the capital of Serbia, a few days after Ratko Mladic had been captured by the Serbian police. Ratko Mladic, also known as one of the Butchers of Bosnia, was accused of orchestrating the largest mass murder in Europe since World War II and had evaded capture for sixteen years. The city was on edge as Mladic's ultra-right-wing supporters rallied in front of the Parliament building in support of their hero. He was to be flown to the International Criminal Court to stand trial for his crimes. I participated in a conference with the Minister of Justice, the person responsible for Mladic's capture and extradition, who spoke of the need to include LGBT people in the human rights system in Serbia. She delivered her words from behind a podium flanked by armed guards in uniform. The man sitting casually in the seat in front of me holding a gun at his waist was one of many plainclothes guards who also surrounded the minister. This high government official easily spoke of LGBT rights, but only from a well-fortified position.

The Serbian gay pride celebration of 2010 became a symbol of the complete disconnect between the legal standard and the reality. By presidential decree, the marchers received official protection against right-wing mobs. A section of the capital was emptied of traffic and 5,000 police were assigned to protect the marchers. Right-wing mobs attacked with Molotov cocktails, bricks and glass bottles. The police defended with rubber bullets and tear gas. Eventually the celebrants had to escape the event and take on right-wing extremists in order to return home. By the end of the day, an unknown number of

LGBT people were brutally beaten, and 150 police were treated for injuries. This experience was by no means one of equality.

After my time in Serbia, I and a few other lawyers and law professors made our way to Montenegro, a small mountainous country bordering Serbia. The Montenegrin government was very supportive of our visit, and assigned several police to escort our group and insure our safety against any possible anti-gay activity. Two weeks before, there had been an attack on an LGBT group's gay pride event when someone threw a tear gas canister into a community theater. The police officer assigned to me at the airport was a massive man who spoke very little English and communicated to me one thing: As we drove past the Christian Orthodox church, he pointed to it, then to himself, and then he swung his finger to indicate the surrounding houses to let me know where I was. This was a Christian country. Then, he pointed to me and the car door and indicated that I was to stay in the car unless he let me out. Those were the rules. The local LGBT population had the benefit of some superlative legal standards, but they did not have armed guards to keep them safe.

Travelling farther down the coast, I ended up in Croatia during the visit of Pope Benedict XVI. He delivered Mass to a crowd equal to one-third the population of the capital. This deeply Catholic nation has a national non-discrimination system that, on paper, is among the best in the world. I saw breathtaking coastlines, peaceful communities, and gorgeous men and women. What I did not see was a broad acceptance of LGBT people to match the broad acceptance of LGBT rights in the law.

The law does not dictate individual action for a variety of reasons. Someone like Ratko Mladic and his brutal followers were criminals and evaded the law. The brave LGBT people who celebrated pride in Serbia remained protected until they stepped outside of the reach of the law. The police officer who protected me dutifully followed his obligation under the law, but he made it clear to me that the law stood side by side with the church. The law in Croatia was generally ignored by the Catholic faithful, whose hearts tied them to their Pope.

The law operates on at least two levels. "De jure" (Latin for according to the law) refers to the legal standard according to the formally recognized written law. "De facto" (Latin for according to the facts) refers to the standard according to the actual practice. Activism aimed at passing laws or seeking precedents from high courts targets the *de jure* law. Serbia and Croatia receive high scores for the state of *de jure* LGBT equality. The *de facto* equality of LGBT people in those countries is very low.

The difference can work the other way. In the United States, laws prohibiting sodomy were commonplace during much of the last century. Nevertheless, many people felt free to engage in sodomy if they wished. As a *de facto* matter, sodomy was permissible in many jurisdictions with anti-sodomy laws.

In Pennsylvania, the domestic violence laws cover same-sex couples. An abused partner has the legal right to seek a restraining order against his or her same-sex batterer on an equal basis. However, many people simply did not know their rights. Others called the police, but the police did not enforce the law properly. Once at the court building, people seeking restraining orders would be required to stand in the waiting room full of other people and shout their story to a court worker sitting behind bullet-proof glass. To add to the usual level of humiliation involved in the process, the LGBT person would have to come out in front of a room full of strangers. For these LGBT people, the *de facto* law did not provide the same protections as the *de jure* law.

The capabilities approach allows us to catapult over the differences between *de jure* and *de facto* law by focusing on how the law actually affects the capabilities of individuals to engage in activities supposedly protected by the law. Rather than asking whether the law, as it is written, protects a person's right to express themselves, the question becomes whether people, given how the law operates, can express themselves.

The differences between de facto and de jure legal standards can be measured. The World Justice Project's Rule of Law Index measures the *de facto* operation of law in several dozen categories including police conduct, government transparency, freedom of thought and religion, access to the court system, independence of judicial systems, and others. A score is assigned for each category, along with a score which indicates how closely the *de facto* law matches the *de jure* law. A committee of experts assigns the scored based on several types of data. First, the laws are analyzed by legal experts. Second, 1,000 people in three cities per country are polled about their experiences with the legal system. Last, a questionnaire about the day-to-day reality of law enforcement and legal practices is sent to law professors, attorneys and law enforcement officials around the country.[105] Similar indices of democracy and governance are produced by Freedom House and other organizations.[106]

Quantitative comparisons such as these can tell us whether people are actually experiencing the equality required by legal standards. These data gathering efforts can document the lived experience of individuals in a variety of sectors. These scores can help prioritize which issues should receive attention by those with limited resources.

Promoting Rights
Important to LGBT People

CHOICE AND CONSENT. The capabilities approach aligns well with the priorities of the LGBT movement because it embraces the principles of consent, choice, and autonomy. A capability is defined as the opportunity to choose something. Freedom of choice has been a highly important and contested issue for LGBT people. Because LGBT people have had gender roles and sexual norms forced on them, being able to exercise choice and consent is a core component of the LGBT agenda. The debate about sending teenagers to conversion therapy comes down to whether a parent will permit a child to express themselves and form relationships in a certain way. Feminists have incorporated the notion of choice into the LGBT agenda by seeking respect for alternative family arrangements that deviate from the traditional marital household.

Under the capabilities approach, knowing whether someone has chosen the activities in their life helps us evaluate the value of those activities to that person. Is someone doing something because they had choices and a good process or were their options limited? Say, for instance, a transgender man with a child is working a series of seasonal jobs in the building and construction industry. We know that he presents himself in a way that is considered masculine, and his job record shows that he has periods of long hours interspersed with periods of little work.

If we knew that his professional circumstance was due to lack of options, we might conclude that he was not leading the kind of life he wanted. He may have been shut out of other kinds of employment because of his gender non-conforming appearance. Possibly he has to take any job available to support himself and his child. He has no personal relationships with co-workers and little opportunity for advancement, but he shows up and is a reliable worker. If he misses work, he will be fired, and he takes any cyclical work he can get.

On the other hand, we might conclude something very different if we learn that he was attracted to carpentry and construction at a young age and is doing exactly what he has always wanted to do. Possibly, he had a desk job but was more attracted to the outdoor and physical activity in the construction industry. The fact that the work is seasonal permits him to be with his child when school is out. The pay is good enough to equal what he would have made at a 9 to 5 office position. Understanding why he chose this job leads us to a very different conclusion about what we should do to change or support his life's activities.

HUMAN RIGHTS. On December 10, 2011, U.S. Secretary of State Hillary Clinton travelled to the UN Human

Rights Council to make a keynote address in which she declared, "gay rights are human rights, and human rights are gay rights."[107] The occasion of this address was the anniversary of the signing of The Universal Declaration of Human Rights, a simple document of thirty articles, each about one sentence long. It includes many of the rights similar to those in the U.S. Constitution, including the rights to vote, to have privacy, to be equal under the law, to be given fair trial, to associate, and to worship. Many other rights go beyond the commonly accepted legal standards in the US, including the right to work, to receive an education, to have the highest attainable level of healthcare and housing, to share in cultural and scientific advances, and others. Since the signing of the Universal Declaration, many subsequent treaties have been adopted by groups of countries, each treaty focusing on a particular set of rights. The United States has signed or ratified treaties concerning torture, race discrimination, and refugee rights. Other countries have also entered into treaties dealing with the rights of children, people with disabilities, and women, economic rights, and others.

All these documents collectively comprise what Hillary Clinton was calling human rights. Clinton's point was that LGBT people have the same sets of rights as any other group.

In 2007, a group of international human rights experts gathered in Yogyakarta, Indonesia, to answer the question "what are the obligations of governments to LGBT people under currently accepted human rights law." These experts included the former UN High Commissioner for Human Rights, high UN officials in the areas of children's rights, civil and political rights, summary executions, health, and torture, as well as leading legal thinkers from Asia, Africa, Europe, and NGO activists. The result was an historic document, which became known as the Yogyakarta Principles on the Application of International Human Rights Law in Relation to Sexual Orientation and Gender Identity, or simply the Yogyakarta Principles. This group of people (after extensive preparations leading up to the conference) spent days walking through each area of international human rights law and applying it to sexual orientation and gender identity issues.[108]

I was extraordinarily privileged to attend that meeting in my capacity as chair of the International Human Right Funders Group. The participants captured a list of currently existing rights that was most important to LGBT people. The Yogyakarta Principles identify roughly thirty sets of rights, including equality, recognition of identity, security of the person, privacy, work, adequate standard of living, adequate housing, the highest attainable standard of health, protection from medical abuses, freedom of opinion, expression, assembly, association, conscience, religion, movement, participation in public and cultural life, and others. In each area, the principles set out the current standard as well as make recommendations to governments. Some of these rights, such as freedom from arbitrary execution, are fairly absolute. Some, such as the right to health, are progressively realizable, depending on a government's ability to provide them. Nonetheless, all people hold these rights, as they are universal. The principles have been publicly referenced by UN officials and officials from nearly 40 governments as an authoritative definition of the rights held by LGBT people.[109]

Most of the rights identified in the Principles are captured by the list of capabilities. More importantly, the capabilities approach provides a method to operationalize human rights. While the analysis of so-called "negative" rights, such as privacy, expression, and non-discrimination, has become familiar and well developed, the "positive" rights have presented more of a challenge. At issue is how to precisely calibrate the obligation of a government given fiscal and resource constraints. Healthcare, education, and social security all require trade-offs, as do many human rights. The capabilities approach focuses on improvements that are within reach. The approach gets to the heart of the issue of improving human rights by asking how we can increase a person's enjoyment of specific rights.

ADDRESSING MULTIPLE DIFFERENCES. LGBT people develop along different paths than non-LGBT people. However, not all LGBT people develop along the same path. Differences in race, gender, class, education, geography, and other experiences operate in ways that are deeply and powerfully determinative of a person's capabilities. Traditionally, some LGBT groups have attempted to form agendas that focus on LGBT identities and ostensibly stay neutral with regard to other identities. Even today some argue that issues such as marriage equality or employment non-discrimination based on sexual orientation and gender identity are 'race-neutral' priorities. Such a views falls in line with much of American identity politics and draws a line around one identity while ignoring the lines drawn by other kinds of differences. For the LGBT movement this approach assumes the movement can dismantle bias against LGBT people without having to confront bias against people of color, women, or the poor.

This strategy of confronting one bias at a time is attractive because it is perceived to be more efficient and viable than confronting multiple biases. It assumes that because each bias applies to a different characteristic, each bias must be constructed one at a time. Efforts to dismantle a single bias will produce a better return on investment with a lower risk of failure than efforts to dismantle multiple biases. Indeed, policy changes in the past decade could serve as evidence that progress on LGBT rights moves at a separate pace, independent from progress on issues of race and gender.

Such an attachment to a "one-identity at a time" approach has three major problems. First, the assumption that the biases are separate may simply be wrong. Preferences for white people, straight people, and male people may arise from the same set of sources. Second, such an approach may produce hidden or deferred costs of fully eliminating bias. If LGBT advocacy efforts are undertaken without examining other prejudices that are operating, then those efforts may themselves reaffirm and repeat those prejudices. The capacity of the LGBT movement to confront anti-LGBT bias is itself affected by systems of racism and sexism that affect all other American political and social systems. The result will be a movement that is more effective at confronting anti-LGBT bias for white people than for black people or for men than for women or for gender conforming people than for transgender people.

The lived experiences of lesbians, people of color, and transgender people tell us that when this happens, the excluded group still faces anti-LGBT bias. The efforts to bring more workers into an anti-gay workplace may result in a workplace that prefers white LGBT people to black LGBT people, or a school that protects the queer kids, but only ones who speak English. In this case, the full costs of eliminating bias against LGBT people are hidden and deferred until future efforts finally address the bias faced by those in the excluded group. Thus, the ultimate return on the investment of these efforts may be limited if all biases are not taken into account.

Finally, even if biases are caused by different sets of prejudices and can be separately enumerated, the required remedy may be one that responds simultaneously to multiple biases at once. For example, say an owner of a trailer park refuses to accept a gay man's application for a rental space because he thinks gay men party too much, and the same owner refuses to rent to an African-American man because he thinks African-Americans might be too violent. The response to each incident of bias would be to seek to require the owner to treat all applicants according to the merits of the application, their timeliness, make sure they had the appropriate licenses, and so on. In cases where the remedy sought by LGBT advocates is to have the owner (or an employer or a librarian or an intake person at a social service agency) make decisions according to the relative merits applicable to that decision, then the more coherent goal is to confront all biases that are inconsistent with a merit-based decision. It does not matter that the biases are independently created. Arguing for a rational remedy of one bias and not another is itself incoherent.

On a sweeping scale, the equality clause adopted in the 1994 constitution in South Africa, along with clauses that granted a series of general human rights, recognized that the only way to coherently disassemble anti-black bias in apartheid-era South Africa was to formally confront the broad range of biases in place in South Africa at that time. On a smaller scale, this is often the approach in the U.S. when a court issues a decree that seeks to insure that an institution does not act according to any bias but makes decisions based on appropriate standards. In these types of cases, the more efficient and effective response is to seek rationality for everyone rather than carve out a response solely for LGBT people.

The capabilities approach cuts through the layers of identity and looks at individuals in ways that are as individualized as possible. The analysis only works if it examines all the aspects of LGBT people's lives that affect development, including race, ethnicity, and class. Employing the capabilities approach in a color-blind way would simply be incompetent. For example, if an LGBT group that focuses on safety finds that black LGBT people experience higher rates of police misconduct than white LGBT people, then any response would need to address the racial aspect of the problem. If it doesn't, then the program will only be partially effective.

The capabilities approach is also useful because it values an individual's ability to develop their identity as they wish. It does not pre-determine the kind of identity, sexuality, or gender one should adopt. Therefore, the young transgender man's identity is just as valuable as that of the young woman who wants to live according to traditional gender roles. The capabilities approach says people must have the capability to join a community, but it does not dictate what kind of community they should join. It says people must have the capability to learn and worship but leaves the decision of what they learn and worship up to them. Because it measures capability rather than actual functioning, it permits variation in sexuality and gender.

-6-

New Visions
for LGBT Advocacy

Building a movement to support the well-being of individual LGBT people will require new programs and priorities. First, the new movement would focus on LGBT people and populations rather than on institutions and governments. Second, such a movement would place a premium on understanding the lived experiences of LGBT people. Research and data analysis would be a core element. Additionally, I propose the creation of an American LGBT well-being index to track the status of the progress of LGBT people in the United States. This section explores each of these themes.

Continue Battle
for Legal Equality

The capabilities approach requires that irrational limitations placed on individuals because of sexual orientation and gender identity be eliminated. Additionally, the capabilities approach requires institutions to treat individuals with dignity. Unequal treatment because of sexual orientation or gender identity can constitute a violation of dignity. Placing categorical restrictions on an individual impairs their ability to live in dignity with others. The current equality agenda is a well-developed and successful component of the capabilities approach. The movement should continue its work to seek equality.

Shift Focus from
Institutions to Individuals

A society should be judged not by its institutions but by the kind of lives people live. Institutions are a means to an end. A people-centered approach to LGBT well-being focuses on individual members of the community. Such an approach can be applied to any of the goals that have been adopted by the LGBT community. I will explore three areas to illustrate the difference between an institution-focused approach and an approach focused on the capabilities of individuals people: 1) School safety, 2) identity documentation, and 3) workplace fairness.

In the late 1990s, Jamie Nabozny was a high school student in Ashland, Wisconsin. He realized he was gay in seventh grade. For years, he was relentlessly harassed by fellow students. He was urinated on, mock raped in front of others, and beaten and kicked so hard in the stomach that he required surgery. He complained regularly to his guidance counselor and school administrators, who told him that he should expect such behavior. After attempting suicide twice, he ran away from home in order to avoid going back to school.

He eventually sued his school and was represented by Lambda Legal Defense and Education Fund. The lawsuit resulted in a settlement for Nabozny as well as a precedent-setting judicial opinion that said that a school could be held accountable for not stopping anti-gay abuse. The case was a major success and affected the attitude of educators across the country. The language of the decision was strongly grounded in an equality argument. The court made it clear that neither the level of abuse inflicted on Nabozny nor its effect on his well-being was the question. Rather, the question was whether the school "singled-out a particular group for disparate treatment" and did so "for the purpose of causing .... adverse effects on the identifiable group."[110] Thus, the inquiry did not center on a person—Nabozny—it centered on the institution—the school.

Achieving this equality victory was part of the needed social change. But equal treatment by schools is not enough. A bad school may be equally ineffective and equally unsafe for both LGBT and non-LGBT students. In this case, even though LGBT students have technical equality, they are still getting a bad education. The fact that LGBT students are not able to reach their full potential should be a concern of the LGBT movement regardless of whether equality is in place.

The mission of the Gay Lesbian Straight Education Network (GLSEN) reflects elements of a capabilities approach. GLSEN's articulated mission is to ensure safe schools. Its programs seek more than equal levels of safety. The mission demands actual safety for all students. The National School Climate Survey is a good example of a study that looks at how anti-LGBT prejudice and stigma affect the capability of all students. The survey gathers information from LGBT and non-LGBT students about their experiences in school and analyzes the effects that harassment and violence have on their well-being. The School Climate Survey relies on data concerning student well-being to evaluate the effectiveness of school programs.[111]

Taking the capabilities approach further, we would also look at data about the impact of school safety policies on other issues experienced by the students, such as discipline. There are indications that across the board zero-tolerance anti-bullying policies may have harmful effects on LGBT students. Some data suggests that administrators use these policies to increase expulsion levels for LGBT and non-LGBT students, exacerbating educational barriers and increasing the chances that youth will be on a school to prison trajectory. One can more deeply evaluate such policies by looking at these policies from the perspective of the students.

Choosing one's own identity is not only a fundamental human right but also a basic component of identity development. While formal recognition of gender may be supported in some circumstances, there is no rational need to place gender markers on records where a person's name is sufficient for purposes of identification, such as monthly bus passes, retail shopping cards, and voter identification records. Living with a passport, a driver's license, a social security record, or a birth certificate that indicates a gender that is inconsistent with a person's life can lead to harassment and exclusion from the services that are implicated by the gender marker document.

An approach focused on institutions would seek policies that permit people to affirmatively apply to change their gender. The capabilities approach would examine the impact of gender marker requirements on the capabilities of voting, engaging economically as a consumer, accessing health care, and so on. Furthermore, the capabilities approach would ask whether individuals are seeking gender marker changes and if not, why not. These approaches are complementary and, used together, would yield a more thorough improvement in the lives of transgender people.

Similarly, let's consider the problem of employment discrimination. An institutional policy approach would focus on seeking LGBT-friendly workplaces. A capabilities approach would ask whether LGBT people can get a job. The Human Rights Campaign regularly publishes reports on LGBT equality in corporate America, such as the State of the Workplace Report, the Corporate Equality Index, and the LGBT Buyers Guide. As part of these reports, HRC asks corporations what policies they have adopted to ensure equality, and then HRC scores corporations based on their answers. These reports have been enormously useful tools in pressuring companies to respond. However, these reports do not ask LGBT people about their experiences as workers. They tell us very little the capabilities of LGBT workers.

Out and Equal Workplace Advocates, a national LGBT organization dedicated to creating safe and equitable workplaces, recommends the use of anonymous workplace climate surveys. Such surveys ask workers themselves whether diversity policies are helping them obtain and keep their jobs. Other methods of analyzing workplaces, such as looking at the experiences of applicants and comparing the proportion of LGBT people in a workplace to the proportion of LGBT people in a corresponding labor market, would also help measure whether anti-LGBT bias is present in employers' decisions.

The capabilities approach would also focus on the workplace skills of LGBT people themselves. Services and Advocacy for GLBT Elders (SAGE) runs SAGE-Works, a national work readiness program for lesbian, gay, bisexual, and transgender mature workers (ages 40 and older) who need or want to return to the workplace. The SAGEWorks program helps seniors seeking employment by providing training, employment resources, and general job hunting know-how to support job and financial security. The outcome of the program is to increase the capabilities of seniors to find and retain a job. For transgender people, the National Transgender Discrimination Survey recommends career counseling and job entry assistance for transgender people completing college so that the rates of employment will increase.[112]

A capabilities approach can also be used to refine the legislative agenda of the LGBT community. In the case of employment discrimination, an equality approach would ask whether laws result in changes in employer practices. To answer this question, one might look at hiring patterns of employers to see whether they were making hiring decisions in an unbiased way. A capabilities approach would shift that concern to whether such a law increases the capability of an LGBT person to obtain and retain employment.

A federal law prohibiting employment discrimination against LGBT people, such as the Employment Non-Discrimination Act (ENDA), has been a central priority of the equality agenda. Using a capabilities approach, we would evaluate its effectiveness from the perspective of the worker. Currently, half of all claims of employment discrimination are filed with state agencies rather than the federal agency that would enforce ENDA. The federal agency simply does not have enough offices and workers. For half of the population in Pennsylvania, a 9:00am appointment at the federal office means getting on the road hours before dawn and taking the rest of the day off. Knowing this, and knowing why workers use state rather than federal enforcement mechanisms, may indicate that ENDA is not as far-reaching as hoped. Additionally, ENDA places a limit on certain kinds of monetary claims brought against an employer. Such limitations do not apply to state laws. Lastly, ENDA only applies to employers with fifteen or more employees, whereas many state laws apply to smaller employers. Addressing these concerns, passage of state laws may emerge as a priority of a capabilities agenda.

Include Closeted, Questioning, and Out People

Embedded in a people-centered approach is the assumption that one can identify which people are to be at the center of the movement's activities. However, the LGBT movement is so diverse that it would be difficult for any group to claim that it is serving all LGBT people. In a movement consisting of many organizations, each organization can, and will have to, decide for itself which particular set of individuals it serves.

From the perspective of the larger LGBT movement, the basic question is: Who is in the LGBT community? Demographer Gay Gates of UCLA's Williams Institute was placed at the center of this question in 2011, when he issued a controversial analysis of the LGBT population in the United States.[113] His study was groundbreaking, in that it began to put numbers on claims about population. Gates was credited with saying that 3.8 percent of the U.S. population was LGBT. The number met resistance amongst some LGBT commentators because it was lower than expected. For decades, LGBT leaders have been using the Kinsey ten percent figure. Gates' lower number threatened to decrease the political and cultural relevance of the movement. In fact, the low size of the population became the story itself, as the Associated Press headline reduced it to 1.7 percent (by eliminating transgender people and bisexuals).[114] Some LGBT leaders essentially accused Gates of undermining the community.

In his 2011 report, Gates was entirely transparent about his methodology, averaging the results found by other surveys that asked individuals whether they identified themselves as LGBT and excluding those people who had had same-sex relations or attractions but who did not self-identify. His report did note that 8.2 percent of Americans had engaged in some same-sex sexual behavior, and 11 percent had experienced same-sex sexual attraction. Those who criticized Gates had a problem with the headlines, not the underlying methodology. They saw him as offering a definition of the community that did not comport with theirs. I do not think this is fair to Gates. It ascribes to his study a question that he was not trying to address. The criticism is also intellectually careless. LGBT advocates frequently and effectively analyze data underlying headlines in order to tell a more complete story. The Gates study lays it all out for advocates to do the same.

Subsequent uses of the Gates study have gone beyond the headlines to look to the actual data. When gathering data to address a particular problem, the key to choosing an appropriate definition is to first determine why the data is needed. If the problem is about problems dealing with sexual health, then the definition should include anyone who has engaged in same-sex sexual behavior. If the problem is about exclusion of openly lesbian women, then the definition might be narrower.

Setting aside specific data gathering needs, the dispute raises the question: Who is the LGBT community? When we draw a circle around all the subgroups that are served by all the groups in the movement, who is in and who is not? Does someone count if they engage in same-sex activity but do not self-identify? Is Larry "wide-stance" Craig, the Senator from Idaho who was caught having sex with men in an airport bathroom, a member of the LGBT community? When Jodie Foster came out at the 2013 Academy Awards ceremony, she was heavily criticized for not coming out earlier and more definitively. Is the closet an identity? Are men in opposite sex relationships who refer to themselves as gay "on the down low" part of the community? Jack and Ennis, the cowboy lovers in the Ang Lee film *Brokeback Mountain* both decided not to come out. Are they part of the community? Data show large numbers of bisexuals in America yet the websites of LGBT groups rarely include narratives of bisexuality. Are bisexuals part of the movement?

In many ways, coming out is seen as the requirement for membership in the LGBT community. Ellen Degeneres used to joke about the days when you could open an account at a bank and get a free appliance, and when she came out in 1994, in the world's most orchestrated coming out moment, she joked that now she was part of the club and was waiting for someone to give her a toaster. For every out person, there is another person who is not out but whose behavior and/or attractions place them in the LGBT category. Some of these people may be in the closet for reasons we want to eliminate. Some may be on a chosen life trajectory that does not lead them to an out LGBT identity. For this subset, the equality agenda has a different level of salience. This subset will not see themselves reflected in the movement's organizations. For them, the ability to work as an openly LGBT person or enter into a same-sex marriage may be more theoretical than personal.

Matters of gender identity and expression are equally complex. For me, the word "gender" includes many gender options. However, it is difficult to capture all these different points when administering surveys limited to a few questions. How does data collection reflect our definition of our community? What about the person who, after transitioning from one gender to another, ceases to identify as transgender altogether? Or the man who cross-dresses at home but wears traditional suits at work? What about a woman who maintains a masculine appearance but does not seek to alter her body? This complexity requires us to look at capabilities broadly. The capabilities approach allows us to look at one set of people for purposes of asking questions about work or housing and another set of people with regard to family or education.

I propose that data gathering efforts include self-identified people as well as other people who have felt same-sex attraction, engaged in same-sex behavior, identified their gender in ways that do not match the expectations that correlate to their birth gender, and people who feel they have faced prejudice based on their gender nonconformity (regardless of expressed gender). If our concern is the liberty and well-being of people of all sexual orientations and gender identities, then that concern would lead us to preserve the capabilities of all people to live life anywhere along the spectrum of visibility and recognition. Second, even if particular advocates are more concerned with one subset of the community over another, we want to make sure that each person's expression of their sexuality and gender identity is a result of a genuine choice and not a result of stigma and limited options.

Ask the Question

Effective response to the needs of individuals requires information about those individuals. Though this might state the obvious, knowledge about LGBT people has often been out of reach, requiring advocates and service providers to fill in the blanks on questions of need and effectiveness. For good reasons, the movement has traditionally exercised caution and restraint when considering asking individuals about their sexual orientation and gender identity. In recent years, LGBT people have been increasingly studied as consumers, voters, targets of social service programs, immigrants, parents, and students. Continued advocacy for data collection is a component of the capabilities approach.

Stigma associated with information can decrease the accuracy of the results and endanger the subjects of the data gathering effort. Let us take, for example, an adolescent who has found herself in the care of a family service agency. Possibly she has had to leave her home, and she arrives in the waiting room of a foster care agency. At some point, a social worker will have to evaluate and try to understand what is going on with this young person. The social worker probably has some type of survey or assessment form to complete. Here, these two strangers must sit and, in a few minutes time, discuss deeply personal matters. The youth may be in crisis, scared, tired, and disoriented. The social worker may be backlogged and have little training on LGBT issues.

Should the social worker ask the young girl if she identifies as a lesbian? The youth may fear disclosing. Maybe the youth is in a same-sex relationship but identifies as straight. The youth may use a label that is different than "lesbian," or possibly the issue is gender conformity. Should the worker ask about feelings of attraction or sexual behavior instead? The source of conflict in the youth's life may not be orientation or gender identity at all, even if that was the basis of ill-treatment by others.

If issues concerning the youth's sexual orientation and gender identity surface, should they be recorded in the file? Will such information be helpful to a social worker, who needs to know how to provide good social support for her? Will she be re-stigmatized if her file ends up being read by care-givers or judges who are hostile to her sexual orientation or gender identity? Employers face similar complications in the workplace. Should employers ask each worker to identify their own sexual orientation and gender identity? It is easy to see how stigma can prevent data gathering and, in fact, make the situation worse.

Although these are good concerns, they are not reasons to give up on gathering data. Researchers all over the world are working through problems of this nature and gathering increasingly larger volumes of data about LGBT people. For example, a coalition of foster-care providers has issued guidelines for managing information related to the sexual orientation and gender identity of youth.[115] These guidelines seek to anticipate risks for the youth and prioritize safety, support, and well-being of the child. Out and Equal Workplace Advocates has engaged in a similar effort. The Self-ID Community of Practice includes representatives from corporations and non-profits in the U.S. and Canada. This group has issued similar guidelines on how to gather information in the workplace.[116] Both of these are examples of how principles of data gathering are developed in cooperation with those active in the community and with the best interests of LGBT people in mind.

Other larger efforts demonstrate the current possibilities of data. Gallup, one of the world's largest data-gathering organizations, recently released a report based on a sample of 120,000 interviews, showing us a deeper picture of the community countering many assumptions.

- Non-whites and younger Americans are more likely to identify as LGBT than white or older Americans.
- Americans with lower levels of education are more likely than their higher educated counterparts to identify as LGBT.
- LGBT women are as likely as non-LGBT women to be raising children.[117]

Many government agencies, particularly those dealing with health, have included LGBT populations in their efforts.[118] The National Health Interview Survey and the

National Health and Nutrition Examination Survey collect data on the diet and health of Americans. The National Survey of Family Growth is conducted by the Centers for Disease Control each year to provide reliable national data on marriage, divorce, contraception, and infertility in the United States. This survey asks the respondent about sexual practices, sexual attraction, and whether they identify themselves as heterosexual, homosexual, bisexual, or some other category. The Department of Justice's National Crime Victimization Study is the primary source of information on criminal victimization. This study reports the likelihood of victimization by certain crimes for the population as a whole, as well as for segments of the population. Data collection includes asking individuals whether they feel they have been subjected to crime based on sexual orientation and a number of other characteristics. In the Violence Against Women Survey, respondents are queried about threats, emotional abuse, and violence experienced by marital and cohabitating partners. This survey has been one of the primary sources for studying violence in same-sex relationships.

The Youth Risk Behavior Survey was developed by the Centers for Disease Control in 1990 to monitor causes of death, disability, and social problems among youth and adults in the United States. These causes, often occurring in early childhood, include substance use, physical abuse, alcohol and other drug use, sexual behaviors that lead to unintended pregnancy and sexually transmitted diseases (including HIV infection), and violence and injury. Though the data is compiled and used at the national level, the survey itself is administered by local agencies. These agencies have experimented with different approaches to gathering data. Some have asked whether a youth identifies themselves as gay, lesbian, or transgender, and some have asked whether the youth has experienced feelings of attraction to others of the same-sex, whether the youth currently identifies themselves as the same gender of their birth, or whether they have had sexual or intimate relations with someone of the same sex. Each of these methods of inquiry will yield different results.

The U.S. Equal Employment Opportunity Commission and the Bureau of Labor Statistics collect data about minorities in the workplace. Each year large employers must file an "EEO-1" form, quantifying the number of certain racial, ethnic, and religious minorities in the workforce.[119] During the past decade, most versions of the Employment Non-Discrimination Act, a bill that would prohibit discrimination based on sexual orientation and gender identity, have also prohibited data collection regarding LGBT people. For years, many in the movement were supportive of such a prohibition, fearing the privacy implications of such a data collection effort. Recently, however, advocates have developed data collection methods to respond to such concerns, guided in part by successful examples of how to collect data about HIV infection rates in healthcare systems. The movement's position on this provision of ENDA should change, as LGBT people will be left out unless they are counted.

The U.S. Department of Health and Human Services sponsored a project to determine the research needs of LGBT populations. In 2014, this project concluded that a number of research efforts was needed to fully under-stand the reasons for disparities and the needs for more services. More sources of data are needed, it concluded, to understand whom among LGBT populations are at greatest risk for poor economic outcomes. Ultimately, the project concluded that government agencies needed to know what kinds of services are needed to respond to the specific circumstances of LGBT people and produce a genuine increase in the well-being of LGBT people.[120]

An American LGBT Development Index

Using the capabilities approach, the LGBT movement will need to identify what kinds of improvements it wishes to achieve in the lives of LGBT people. Ideally, the goals would be stated in terms of specific lived experience of LGBT people. For example, programs run by governments and LGBT groups might seek to " 'reduce health disparities experienced by transgender elders by thirty percent' or 'eliminate the wage gap faced by lesbians' or 'cut in half the incidence of self-reported harassment by students' or 'ensure that LGBT people vote at the same rate as others.' "

Currently, many such programs exist in the LGBT community to improve the lives of community members. However, only recently has the community begun to have the tools to conduct the kinds of measurements that are needed to determine whether such programs are successful. As the movement begins to expand its focus on improving individual lives, it needs to more frequently employ tools to evaluate which programs worked and which did not.

As a step toward promoting a community-wide awareness of the lived experience of LGBT people, I propose that the movement create an American LGBT development index. Such an index can be used to track the progress of LGBT well-being, to set priorities for additional work, as well as serve to show how such measurements are conducted. As I propose it, the index would be a set of measurements developed in consultation with affected members of the LGBT community. The term index, used in this way, is not one number but is actually a collection of measurements, each detailing the condition of LGBT people in a variety of categories. Once established, such measurements could be used in local communities across the country to identify needs, evaluate the effectiveness of laws and programs, and communicate priorities of LGBT people.

The process of developing an index would have to include people and groups in the affected communities. What to measure, how to measure, and who to measure are all questions that can not be answered without consulting LGBT people themselves. A possible set of issues might correspond to the list of capabilities that we all feel are important to a better life:

- Physical and mental health
- Safety from violence
- Happiness and social support
- Education
- Civil participation
- Expression of identity
- Employment
- Parenting and coupling
- Finances
- Housing

Such a set of measurements could be applied to youths, elders, by race and ethnicity, state and region, income level, and so on. Such a set could also be applied to people who self-identified as gay, lesbian, or bisexual, as well as those who have experienced same-sex attraction or sexual encounters but do not self-identify and to categories of people according to gender identity.

Numbers are taken seriously, and the process of establishing an index would require significant thought, expertise, and community cooperation. LGBT groups would need to understand that creating the standards and criteria for such a set of measurements is as time-consuming as conducting the measurements. In the same way that a building is constructed for many years of occupancy, an index would need to be designed for many years of use.

Like the human development index, a composite indicator could express, in a single number, the development of the larger LGBT community. Such a single number could help communicate trends and comparisons. This index would communicate the message that in America there is a real, measurable population of individuals facing impediments to full opportunity and development. An index would illustrate that these conditions are identifiable and actionable. Such an index could be issued on an annual basis and could be used as a media tool by LGBT groups for public awareness and advocacy.

-7-

LGBT People are Good

"Gay is Good," said Frank Kameny, co-founder of the Mattachine Society, and one of the parents of the contemporary gay rights movement. Several years before the Stonewall riots, Kameny was already organizing rallies in front of the White House and Independence Hall. The annual Reminder Marches, held on July 4th in front of Independence Hall in Philadelphia, were to remind the American public that a certain percentage of the population was denied life, liberty, and the pursuit of happiness. The capability approach attempts to complete this promise for LGBT people. Individuals should have not only the freedom to live but also the tools to pursue a better life.

In 1957, Kameny was fired by the Army from his job as an astrophysicist after the Army discovered he had been arrested for making a sexual advance on an undercover police officer. Soon thereafter, Kameny started meeting with other gay men to begin political organizing in what was known as the homophile movement. As an activist, Kameny paired his claim for equality with an assertion of the essential goodness of each person. He coined the phrase "Gay is Good," taking a cue from the slogan "Black is Beautiful" being used in the black civil rights movement at that time. Kameny deliberately sought to imbue his slogan with a moral judgment. He wanted to directly respond to the claims of those who sought to use morality against gay people. Kameny said "homosexuality is not only *not* immoral but is affirmatively moral"[121]

I met Kameny in the late eighties. He was a regular participant at legal events in Washington, DC, when I was the co-chair of GAYLAW, the lesbian and gay bar association, and he eventually became involved in an activist reading group that my partner and I hosted in our apartment. Kameny had one, singular position from which he never deviated, and which he always delivered with a granite-splitting voice: Gay (eventually LGBT) people are good. They are full citizens with human rights. Period. The rest follows from that.

I came to deeply admire Kameny's clarity. At the very beginning of the movement, he had already arrived at the end point of LGBT advocacy. His perspective places people at the center of the debate over rights. Actions of governments and organizations only matter insofar as they can support people.

The capabilities approach imagined in this book seeks a society where LGBT people can strive for a better life. In such a society, the choice to live openly as LGBT, with all the variations that might entail, would be as equally worthy as any other choice. Governments and communities would affirm and support the ability of all people to set their own path. Public agencies would devote resources to programs targeted toward LGBT populations. Legislatures would support laws not just to remove barriers for LGBT people, but to actively promote their well-being. LGBT people would have not just equality, but affirmative support and approval. In short, such a society would value LGBT people and the choices they make.

It is possible that such a society might be achievable if everyone adheres to a live-and-let-live set of social rules. However, this path seems naïve, given the amount of daily prejudice and stigma still faced by LGBT people every day. I think that Americans will not support the capability of all LGBT people to pursue a better life until there is a fuller understanding of the lived experience of LGBT people and a broader agreement that LGBT people are as worthy, as good, as decent, and as moral as anyone else.

The LGBT movement is becoming more fluent in the language of values and morality (I use these terms interchangeably in this discussion). However, this has not always been the case. Avoiding issues of morality and values has been a part of LGBT advocacy tacticsfor many years. This tactic, labeled "moral bracketing," has been employed by many political advocates. The tactic entails placing a bracket around moral disputes and seeking agreement on neutral issues. Moral bracketing is deeply ingrained in American pluralistic political values. It assumes that individuals living in the same community should, to the greatest extent possible, have the liberty to hold different moral views as long as they find some way to get along for the purposes of governance and meeting common needs. It accepts a distinction between beliefs which are manifested in a personal, private sphere, and beliefs which may invoke benefits or harms to others.

Arguments by the LGBT community against sodomy laws often employed moral bracketing. For example, in 1999, legal groups brought a challenge to the Texas sodomy law on behalf of John Lawrence and Tyrone Gardner, both of whom had been convicted of sodomy. The challenge was based on two arguments. First, the equality argument—the laws treated gay people and gay sex differently than straight people and straight sex. Second, the privacy argument—the law violated "liberty protections that the Constitution erects in order to preserve a private sphere shielded from government intrusion."[122] LGBT groups did not talk much about sodomy, the activity that took place behind that shield.

Supporters of the sodomy laws felt very comfortable talking about sodomy. Primarily, they argued that it was morally bad and that its moral qualities would negatively impact larger society. Some supporters of the sodomy laws also catalogued supposedly negative physical and psychological consequences of gay sex. LGBT advocates never fully engaged in a discussion of why sex between two men was as morally worthy as sex between a man and a woman. Nor did they argue that same-sex sexual activity can contribute to well-being and healthy personal development, particularly for LGB people. LGBT advocates stuck to arguments about equality and privacy. The tactic paid off. In 2003, the U.S. Supreme Court struck down the Texas sodomy law.

Keeping morality out of policy decisions may be a hallmark of liberal political advocacy, but the American conservative movement discarded the tactic years ago. In 1992, Patrick Buchannan reinvigorated the culture wars when he opened the Republican National Convention with a speech condemning gay and lesbian rights and people who would support them. He claimed that George Bush had the moral authority to lead the country, and its armed forces, because Bush opposed gay couples, women in combat, and judicial activism. Morality was a winning argument for the Republicans, as well as many Democrats. From the mid-seventies through 1992, two-thirds to three-quarters of Americans said that homosexual behavior was always wrong.[123]

However, during that same period, eighty percent of Americans though that gay and lesbian people should have equal rights in the workplace. A significant number of Americans fell into the moral bracket: they felt opposed to homosexuality on moral grounds, but they did not support jailing or firing gay people from their jobs. They felt sympathetic to the principles of tolerance and fairness. This moveable middle became the target of LGBT advocacy efforts for the next 15 years. As Urvashi Vaid detailed in *Virtual Equality*, a seminal analysis of the LGBT movement, the LGBT community sought to build alliances by taking positions in common with other oppressed minorities. Generally, the community sought to keep morals out of the public square.

In 1998, the conservative groups launched a high profile campaign about the dangers of homosexuality. The campaign featured full page newspaper ads in which ex-gay Ann Paulk told her story of having been made a lesbian. Paulk talked of her conversion from sin to a heterosexual life. Elizabeth Birch, President of the Human Rights Campaign, appeared on Larry King Live to respond to the campaign. Guest host Wolf Blitzer asked Birch "What do you say to the argument that Reverend Jerry Falwell is a theologian, and he is strictly going by what the Bible says about homosexuality." Birch responds with a classic "love the sinner" message:

> "Everyone is a sinner. Reverend Falwell is a sinner. He had a very unruly teenagehood: The fact

> is that those messages [the newspaper ads] miss
> the central point of the scripture, and the central
> message of the scripture is about love, and its
> about unity and not about division and divisive
> messages."[124]

Birch's response represented the best thinking in the movement about how to handle moral arguments. She did not challenge the notion that homosexuals were sinners. She tried to divert the argument away from the morality of homosexuality.

Contrast this exchange with one that took place years later on the Oprah Winfrey show.[125] A member of Oprah's audience called into the show from his home and told Oprah and her guests that his Christian upbringing conflicted with being gay. Reverend Ed Bacon, a guest of Oprah, responded, "Being gay is a gift from God." Oprah exclaimed that she had never heard such a thing from a minister. On a later show, Bacon elaborated that all lesbian and gay people should understand that they are good.

A comparison of these two approaches shows how the moral bracket works. Birch put a bracket around the moral claims and dismissed them in favor of her primary arguments of unity. Bacon responded directly to the moral issue by claiming a positive morality for gay people. The LGBT community continued to employ the moral bracket throughout the debates about employment non-discrimination and marriage.

In California, the effort to stop Proposition 8, which amended the California Constitution to ban same-sex marriage, was based initially on the use of the moral bracket. The campaign took the approach that the "message should deemphasize the impact of the ballot measure on LGBT people and avoid the word 'gay.'"[126]

Instead, the campaign sought to use non-gay endorsers and focus on more general notions of exclusion and worries about changing the state constitution. The hope was that the ballot initiative could be defeated without having to change minds about gay people or gay marriage.

On October 28, 2008, a few days before Californians voted on Proposition 8, the "No on 8" campaign released a television ad featuring Senator Dianne Feinstein. This was one of the most widely distributed ads of the campaign. In the ad Feinstein speaks directly to the camera:

> "In my lifetime, I've seen discrimination. And I see it again in Proposition 8. Proposition 8 would be a terrible mistake for California. It changes our Constitution, eliminates fundamental rights, and treats people differently under the law. Proposition 8 is not about schools or our kids. It's about discrimination and we must always say no to that. No matter how you feel about marriage, vote against discrimination, and vote NO on 8."[127]

In another series of ads targeting Spanish-speaking voters, America Ferrera, a star in the hit series "Ugly Betty," states that "This is not about being gay or straight, it's about being American."[128] In another ad, Sam and Julia Thoron, parents of gay daughter Liz, say "regardless of how anyone feels about marriage for gay and lesbian couples, people should not be singled out for unfair treatment under the laws of our state."[129]

The issue of homosexuality is explicitly avoided in these ads. Feinstein does not use the word "gay," and the other ads say that homosexuality is irrelevant. The issue of marriage is explicitly bracketed by Feinstein's diversionary "no matter how you feel about marriage . . ." The ads give permission to viewers to hold on to their homophobia and personal doubts against gay marriage couples as long as they don't seek to officially discriminate.

Several of the campaigns fighting anti-gay ballot initiatives in other states tried to make common ground on issues other than the capability of gay people to marry. In a Missouri ad, Navy Veteran Damon Hayward assures listeners that their anti-gay morality will be kept safe. "Amendment 2 isn't about gay marriage. That's already banned in Missouri. It's about putting unequal treatment in Missouri's Constitution."[130] Another ad in Florida said "Personal marriage issues should be decided by you, your family, and clergy, not the government. Keep government out of our private lives. Vote No on 2."[131]

Voters approved Proposition 8 in California with roughly the same levels of support and opposition that existed before the campaign. The loss was crushing and was followed by a similar loss in Maine a year later. Following the defeats, LGBT organizations spent significant resources to examine why voters rejected marriage equality. The movement re-engineered its messages.[132] One such evaluation concluded that de-gayed campaigns would not succeed:

> ". . . either allow the opposition to define who gay people are and what we're like and allow their characterization of us as dangerous and untrustworthy to become the dominant understanding in the campaign discourse; or, belatedly, rebut the attacks. Thus far, we have not managed to win under either set of circumstances.[133]

Another evaluation concluded that many voters did not understand why gay and lesbian people sought the capability to marry. Straight Americans said that marriage, for them, was about love, commitment, and responsibility. However, when asked why they thought gay and lesbian people wanted to marry, many said it was for rights and benefits. Gay and lesbian people were perceived as motivated by greed rather than other values considered more worthy.[134] This should come as no surprise. After all, marriage advocates had spent years talking about rights and benefits.

In subsequent years, public education efforts focused explicitly on the values that couples attached to marriage. The capability to marry was placed in a framework of personal ideals. Gay people spoke for themselves, particularly when it came to discussing the meaning of marriage. The values of love and commitment replaced arguments about exclusion and state constitutions. The central strategy statement of Freedom-to-Marry, the primary marriage equality group, said "[t]his shift away from a focus on abstract rights and benefits has been crucial to the exponential growth in support for marriage."[135] As Americans gained a deeper, authentic understanding of LGBT people, their support for building the capabilities of LGBT people increased. The campaigns about love and commitment made LGBT lives more understandable and authentic.

In 2012, after a 32 state losing streak, the people of Maine, Maryland, Washington, and Minnesota voted in support of giving same-sex couples the capability to marry. During the same period, the American public began changing its opinion about lesbian and gay people. The proportion of Americans that believe homosexuality is acceptable has increased throughout the past 20 years. The largest increases occurred after 2008.[136] After examining quantitative and qualitative data, one set of researchers said that the connection between moral disapproval of homosexuality and opposition to marriage equality was "unequivocal."[137]

In the course of implementing the capabilities approach, LGBT groups will have the opportunity to encourage the increasing approval of homosexuality by Americans. The approach will require public discussion

about each of the facets of life that matter to public policy: health, education, work, family, and so on. Each capability is anchored in the lived experience of LGBT people
and reflects the values that LGBT people attach to them.
In the same way that the LGBT movement talked about
marriage through the lenses of love, commitment, and
responsibility, the movement will also be able to talk
about each capability in a values framework. Each of the
capabilities is associated with a set of values and can be
linked to a values framework.

For example, the capability to express one's identity is
a manifestation of the values of truth and honesty. Coming out is an act of truth and honesty. Some LGBT people have come out even though they face potential
hostility, rejection, and violence. Some transgender people
seek to have identity documentation and outward expression match their inner perception of their gender. A lesbian worker may want to be able to talk about her female
partner in the break room in the same way that straight
women talk about male partners. A gay man may want to
be able to tell his doctor or priest about his life without
lying. The community celebrates National Coming Out
Day and provides coming out guides and resources to
those who are struggling with the process.

The lived experiences of LGBT people provide many
permutations on the role of truth and honesty in an individual's life. While these experiences do not make LGBT
more moral than anyone else, they do show that LGBT

people have a moral dimension where values can play a direct and active role in their lives. Talking about these life experiences in a values framework may help bridge gaps in understanding about LGBT individuals in ways that connect to non-LGBT people who share those values. For those who see truth and honesty as a good thing, then it follows that LGBT people should be given the capabilities to follow these values themselves.

The capability to live life free of violence is based in a desire to uphold the values of peace and safety. Most states have an LGBT anti-violence project; many LGBT groups advocate for safe schools, and LGBT groups seek prosecution of perpetrators of hate crimes. LGBT groups themselves seek a strong response to intimate partner violence in same-sex couples. The aspiration to peace and safety is evident at LGBT events. In New York, where I lived for many years, police officers wanted to work during Pride weekend because, among the large scale marches and festivals, Pride had the lowest level of violence and unlawfulness.

The capability to work can be associated with a number of values, including accomplishment and service. Debates about the Don't ask Don't Tell policy highlighted story after story of Americans who wanted to serve their country. The same can be said of gay men who wanted to volunteer for the Boy Scouts and transgender people who have sought to work in law enforcement.

The capability to form family affiliations is based on values of love, commitment, and caring. Before high-profile marriage debates, many lesbians were fighting to keep custody of children they had parented, sometimes with an opposite sex person, sometimes with a lesbian partner. Indeed, organizations and litigators in the movement have strongly advocated for the value of doing what was in the best interests of the child. Other components of the community have valued a variety of different forms of chosen family, from domestic partnerships to co-parenting arrangements to innovative forms of community housing for LGBT elders. Each of these involve varying components of caring, caretaking, and compassion.

Education is tied to the values of self-sufficiency and accomplishment. From a systemic perspective, education and equality are inextricably linked. At a personal level, education may carry different values. Personally, many of my friends who have kids really do not place education in an equality framework. Their main concern is that their children will have sufficient education to be self-sufficient and empowered. Well-being, rather than equality, is the primary long-term value of education. Advancement, earning a living, and seeking a better life are values both LGBT people and non-LGBT people attach to education.

The LGBT community has also demonstrated its commitment to the value of community and contributing to the common good, particularly during times when members of the community were being rejected by others. The history of forming community groups, supporting community centers, and starting LGBT professional associations, have all demonstrated this commitment. Decades ago, the LGBT community had to form a response to HIV/AIDS when gay men were being ignored. The LGBT community has established, through its own funding resources, a network of advocacy organizations. LGBT senior centers are being created by LGBT organizations. These actions reflect a commitment to caring for others in the community.

LGBT people are not simply results of oppression they face. Each person's life experience is more a series of discriminatory events. Rather, each LGBT person's life is an affirmation of choices and capabilities which seek to reach beyond inequality and circumstance. The approaches in this book lift LGBT people out of the dynamics of institutional repression and place them in the process of full acceptance and affirmation. The goal of government, and all social structures, is to continually increase the well-being and capabilities of each person. We should seek no less for LGBT people.

Notes

1. Obergefell v. Hodges, 576 U.S. ____ (2015), 14.

2. Ibid.

3. United States v. Windsor, 133 S. Ct. 2675, 570 US __ (2013).

4. Kenji Yoshino, *Speak Now: Marriage Equality on Trial* (New York: Crown Publishers, 2015) 118.

5. Jules Lobel, Success Without Victory: Lost Legal Battles and the Long Road to Justice in America (New York: New York University Press, 2006).

6. Dale v. Boy Scouts, slip op. A 2427-95T3 (Superior Court of New Jersey, Appellate Division 1998).

7. General Accounting Office, *Defense of Marriage Act Update to Prior Report*, GAO-04-353R (Washington, DC: January 23, 2004),
http://www.gao.gov/new.items/d04353r.pdf.

8. Andrew Park and Tiffany Palmer, *Survey of Statutory Rights Associated with Marriage in Pennsylvania* (Philadelphia: The Center for Lesbian and Gay Civil Rights, Philadelphia, March 23, 1999), 1.

9. Human Rights Campaign, *"Mission Statement,"* Human Rights Campaign website, 2013,
http://www.hrc.org/the-hrc-story/mission-statement.

10. Lambda Legal, *FY 2011-FY2014 Lambda Legal Strategic Plan (New York:* Lambda Legal Defense and Education Fund, 2010),
http://www.lambdalegal.org/sites/default/files/publications/downl
oads/fs_fy-2011-14-lambda-legal-strategic-plan_1.pdf.

11. Barack Obama, quoted in Office of the Press Secretary, President Barack Obama, "Remarks by the President at a Campaign Event, Tampa, FL," The White House website, Secretary, October 25, 2012,
http://www.whitehouse.gov/the-press-office/2012/10/25/remarks-president-campaign-event-tampa-fl.

12. Bowers v. Hardwick, 478 U.S. 186 (1986).

13. Amendment 2, Colo. Const., Art. II, §30b.

14. Brief of Amici Curiae Human Rights Campaign et al. in support of Petitioners, Lawrence and Garner v. Texas, (2003)(Docket no. 2-102), 12-15; Brief of Amici Curiae Constitutional Law Professors in support of Petitioners, Lawrence and Garner v. Texas, (2003)(Docket no. 2-102), 10-16.

15. Gary Gates, *LGBT Parenting in the US* (Los Angeles: The Williams Institute, 2013), http://williamsinstitute.law.ucla.edu/wp-content/uploads/LGBT-Parenting.pdf.

16. Movement Advancement Project, Center for American Progress, and Human Rights Campaign, *A Broken Bargain, Discrimination, Fewer Benefits and More Taxes for LGBT Workers,* (Denver: Movement Advancement Project, 2013), v, http://www.lgbtmap.org/file/a-broken-bargain-condensed-version.pdf.

17. Andras Tilcsik, "Pride and Prejudice: Employment Discrimination against Openly Gay Men in the United States," *American Journal of Sociology* 117, no. 2 (2011): 586-626.

18. Marieka Klawitter, "Multilevel Analysis of the Effects of Antidiscrimination Policies on Earnings by Sexual Orientation," *Journal of Policy Analysis and Management* 30, no. 2 (2011): 334-58.

19. Funder for LGBT Issues, "About Us," Funders for LGBT Issues website, 2014, http://www.lgbtfunders.org/about/index.cfm.

20. Charles Silverstein, "The Religious Conversion of Homosexuals: Subject: Selection is the Voir Dire of Psychological Research" in *Ex-Gay Research Analyzing the Spitzer Study and its Relation to Science, Religion, Politics, and Culture,* eds. Jack Drescher and Kenneth Zucker (New York: Harrington Park Press, 2006), 281-285.

21. Erwin J. Haeberle, "Chronology of Sex Research: II. Pioneers (1896-1936)," *Archive for Sexology wesite,* 2013, http://www.sexarchive.info/GESUND/ARCHIV/CHR06.HTM.

22. A discussion of the causes and effects of the fame of Christina Jorensen can be found in the introduction of her autobiography as well as woven throughout the story of the entire book. Christine Jorgensen, *Christine Jorgensen: A Personal Autobiography* (San Francisco: Cleis Press, 2000).

23. Alfred Kinsey, Wardell Pomeroy, and Clyde Martin, *Sexual Behavior in the Human Male* (Philadelphia: W.B. Saunders Company, 1948), 650-651.

24. Eli Coleman et al., "Standards of Care for the Health of Transsexual, Transgender and Gender Non-Conforming People, Version 7," *International Journal of Transgenderism* 13 (2011): 165-232.

25. Jack Drescher, Peggy Cohen-Kettenis, and Sam Winter, "Minding the Body: Situating Gender Identity Diagnosis in the ICD-11," *International Review of Psychiatry* 26, no. 6 (December 2012): 568-577.

26. The Committee on Nomenclature and Statistics of the American Psychiatric Association, Diagnostic and Statistical Manual: Mental Disorders, Vol. 1 (Washington: American Psychiatric Association Mental Hospital Service, 1952).

27. The Committee on Nomenclature and Statistics of the American Psychiatric Association, Diagnostic and Statistical Manual: Mental Disorders, 2nd ed. (Washington: American Psychiatric Association Mental Hospital Service, 1968).

28. The Committee on Nomenclature and Statistics of the American Psychiatric Association, Diagnostic and Statistical Manual: Mental Disorders, 3rd ed. (Washington: American Psychiatric Association Mental Hospital Service, 1987); American Psychiatric Association, "Position Statement on Homosexuality and Civil Rights," *American Journal of Psychiatry* 131, no. 4 (1974): 497; Jack Drescher, "Gold or Lead? Introductory Remarks on Conversions," in *Ex-Gay Research: Analyzing the Spitzer Study and Its Relation to Science, Religion, Politics, and Culture*, eds. Jack Drescher and Kenneth J. Zucker (New York: Harrington Park Press, 2006), 14.

29. Brief of Amicus Curiae Concerned Women for America in Support of Respondent, Lawrence and Garner v. Texas, 539 U.S. 558 (2003) 22-23.

30. The Committee on Nomenclature and Statistics of the American Psychiatric Association, Diagnostic and Statistical Manual of Mental Disorders, 3rd ed. (Washington, D.C.: American Psychiatric Press, Inc., 1980).

31. Subcommittee on Investigations, Committee on Expenditures in the Executive Departments, Employment of Homosexuals and Other Sex Perverts in Government, 81st Congress, Doc. No. 241 (December 15, 1950), 3-5.

32. Ratchford v. Gay Lib, 434 U.S. 1080, 1084 (1978).

33. Joseph Cardinal Ratzinger, Letters to the Bishops of the Catholic Church on the Pastoral Care of Homosexual Persons, Vatican Web site, http://www.vatican.va/roman_curia/congregations/cfaith/documents/rc_con_cfaith_doc_19861001_homosexual-persons_en.html.

34. Cardinal Zenon Grocholewski, Instruction Concerning the Criteria for the Discernment of Vocations with regard to Persons with Homosexual Tendencies in view of their Admission to the Seminary and to Holy Orders, Vatican Web site, http://www.vatican.va/roman_curia/congregations/ccatheduc/documents/rc_con_ccatheduc_doc_20051104_istruzione_en.html.

35. Sean Lund and Cathy Renna, "An Analysis of the Media Response to the Spitzer Study," in *Ex-Gay Research Analyzing the Spitzer Study and its Relation to Science, Religion, Politics, and Culture*, eds. Jack Drescher and Kenneth Zucker (New York: Harrington Park Press, 2006), 281-285.

36. Historian Allan Berube documents the patterns of migration and economic demand in the introductory chapters of his book. Allan Berube, Coming Out Under Fire (New York: The Free Press, Simon & Schuster Inc., 1990).

37. John D'Emilio, Sexual Politics, Sexual Communities: The Making of a Homosexual Minority in the United States, 1940-1970 (Chicago: University of Chicago Press, 1998), 101-105.

38. Donald Webster Cory, *The Homosexual in America: A Subjective Approach* (New York: Greenberg, 1956), 231-32.

39. Personal interview of George Weinberg, October 30, 1998, cited in Gregory M. Herek, "Beyond 'Homophobia': Thinking about Sexual Prejudice and Stigma in the Twenty-First Century," *Sexuality Research and Social Policy* 1, no.2 (2004): 7.

40. William Dannemeyer, *Shadow in the Land: Homosexuality in America* (San Francisco: Ignatius, 1989), 129.

41. Brook Gladstone, "In Defense of 'Homophobia,'" (includes an interview with George Weinberg), On the Media, December 7, 2012, http://www.onthemedia.org/2012/dec/07/defense-homophobia/transcript/.

42. *Civil Rights Act of 1964* § 7, 42 U.S.C. § 2000e et seq.

43. Herek, "Beyond 'Homophobia,'" 12.

44. Aaron Swartz, "Why I Am Not Gay," Raw Thought Blog, September 8, 2001, http://www.aaronsw.com/weblog/notgay.

45. Brief of Amici Curiae Mary Robinson et al. in support of Petitioners, Lawrence and Garner v. Texas, 539 U.S. 558 (2003) 16, supportively discussing the limiting principles used by Courts in Europe when decriminalizing sodomy. The organizations filing the brief, which include several leading international human rights groups, note that the principles serve as a basis for declining to recognize the legality of commercial sex, even if it takes places in one's home, as well as sado-masochistic sex, even if both parties fully consent.

46. Brief of Petitioner, Lawrence and Garner v. Texas, 539 U.S. 558 (2003).

47. Romer v. Evans, 517 US 620 (1996).

48. *Equal Pay Act of 1963*, 29 U.S.C.A. § 206(b)).

49. U.S. Census Bureau, *Current Population Reports. Income, Poverty, and Health Insurance Coverage in the United States: 2011*, by Carmen De-Navas-Walt, Bernadette D. Proctor, and Jessica C. Smith, P60-243 (Washington, DC: U.S. Government Printing Office, 2012), 9-12.

50. The Fair Housing Act of 1968, 42U.S.C.A. §§ 3601-3631, also known as Title VIII of the Civil Rights Act of 1968.

51. *Title VII of the Civil Rights Act of 1964*, 42 U.S.C.A. § 2000e-4.

52. Urvashi Vaid, Virtual Equality: The Mainstreaming of Gay and Lesbian Liberation (New York: Anchor Books, 1995), 179.

53. Gregory M. Herek, "Beyond Homophobia: Thinking about Sexual Prejudice and Stigma in the Twenty-First Century," *Sexuality Research and Social Policy* 1, no.2 (2004): 6-24.

54. Kenji Yoshino, "Covering," *Yale Lawrence Journal* 111, no.4 (2002) 769; Kenji Yoshino, *Covering: The Hidden Assault on Our Civil Rights* (New York: Random House, 2007).

55. Testimony of Kendall, Perry v. Schwarzeneger (N.D. Calif Jan 20, 2010) (No. 09-2292-VRW), Tr. Vol. 7, p.1522-1544.

56. Chris Hampton, "Why ENDA Matters: True Stories of Anti-LGBT Employment Discrimination from the ACLU," *ACLU: Blog of Rights*, November 3, 2009,

http://www.aclu.org/blog/lgbt-rights/why-enda-matters-true-stories-anti-lgbt-employment-discrimination-aclu.

57. Jamie Grant, Lisa A. Mottet, Justin Tanis, Jack Harrison, Jody L. Herman, and Mara Keisling, *Injustice at Every Turn: A Report of the National Transgender Discrimination Survey* (Washington, DC: National Center for Transgender Equality and National Gay and Lesbian Task Force, 2011), 50-72.

58. Jennifer Pizer, Brad Sears, Christy Mallory, and Nan Hunter, 'Evidence of Persistent Evidence of Persistent and Pervasive Workplace Discrimination Against LGBT People: the Need for Federal Legislation Prohibiting Discrimination and Providing for Equal Employment Benefits,*" Loyola of Los Angeles Law Review* 45, no.3 (2012): 736.

59. Shahar v. Bowers, 114 F.3d 1097, 1101 (11th Cir. 1997) (en banc) (recounting conclusions of lawyers in state attorney general's office that woman's religious same-sex marriage "would create the appearance of conflicting interpretations of Georgia law"); id. at 1107 (endorsing claim of reasonableness of office's conclusion that religious same-sex marriage would likely create "confusion in the minds of members of the public . . . about her marital status").

60. Peter Ringo, "Media Roles in Female-to-Male Transsexual and Transgender Identity Formation," *The International Journal of Transgenderism* 6, no. 3 (2002), http://www.wpath.org/journal/www.iiav.nl/ezines/web/IJT/97-03/numbers/symposion/ijtvo06no03_01.htm#References.

61. Vivienne C. Cass, "Homosexual Identity Formation: Testing a Theoretical Model," *Journal of Sex Research* 20, no. 2 (1984): 143-67.

62. Coleman, 165-232.

63. Aaron H. Devor, "Witnessing and Mirroring: A Fourteen Stage Model of Transsexual Identity Formation," *Journal of Gay and Lesbian Psychotherapy* 8 (2004): 41-67.

64. D.M. Frost and I.H. Meyer, "Internalized Homophobia And Relationship Quality Among Lesbians, Gay Men, And Bisexuals," *Journal of Counseling Psychology*, 56, vol. 1(2009): 97-109.

65. Ilan Meyer, "Prejudice, Social Stress, And Mental Health In Lesbian, Gay And Bisexual Populations: Conceptual Issues And Research Evidence," *Psychological Bulletin* 129, no. 5 (2003): 674-697.

66. Belle Rose Ragins et al., "Making the Invisible Visible: Fear and Disclosure of Sexual Orientation at Work, *J. Applied Psychol.* 92 (2007): 1103-1112.

67. John Pachankis, "The Psychological Implications Of Concealing A Stigma: A Cognitive- Affective-Behavioral Model," *Psychological Bulletin* 133, no.2 (2007): 328-345.

68. Herdt, G. and Boxer, A., *Children of Horizons.* (Boston, MA: Beacon Press, 1996), 205.

69. K. P. Beals, L. A. Peplau, and S. L. Gable, "Stigma Management And Well-Being: The Role Of Perceived Social Support, Emotional Processing, And Suppression," *Personality and Social Psychology Bulletin* 37, no. 7 (2009): 867-879; D. E. S. Frable, L. Platt, and S. Hoey, "Concealable Stigmas And Positive Self-Perceptions: Feeling Better Around Similar Others," *Journal of Personality and Social Psychology* 74, no. 4 (1998): 909-922; T. Frijns, and C. Finkenauer, "Longitudinal Associations Between Keeping A Secret And Psychosocial Adjustment In Adolescence," *International Journal of Behavioral Development* 33 no. 2 (2009): 145-154; E. W. Schrimshaw, K. Siegel, M. J. Downing Jr, and J. T. Parsons, "Disclosure And Concealment Of Sexual Orientation And The Mental Health Of Non-Gay-Identified, Behaviorally Bisexual Men," *Journal of Consulting and Clinical Psychology* 81, no. 1 (2013): 141- 153.

70. M. L. Hatzenbuehler, A. Bellatorre, Y. Lee, B. Finch, P. Muennig, and K. Fiscella, "Structural Stigma And All-Cause Mortality In Sexual Minority Populations," *Social Science and Medicine* 103 (2013): 33-41; D. J. Lick, L. E. Durso, and K. L. Johnson, "Minority Stress And Physical Health Among Sexual Minorities. Perspectives On Psychological Science," 8, no. 5 (2013): 521-548; K. I. Fredriksen-Goldsen, H. J. Kim, and S. E. Barkan, "Disability Among Lesbian, Gay, And Bisexual Adults: Disparities In Prevalence And Risk," *American Journal of Public Health 102*, no. 1 (2011): e16-e21; M. P. Marshal,L. J. Dietz, M. S. Friedman, R. Stall, H. A. Smith, J. McGinley, and D. A. Brent, "Suicidality And Depression Disparities Between Sexual Minority And Heterosexual Youth: A Meta-Analytic Review," *Journal of Adolescent Health* 49, no. 2 (2011): 115-123.

71. Institute for Development Studies, *Sexuality and Development, IDS Policy Briefing* 29, (Brighton: Institute for Development Studies, April 2006); Robert Chambers, "What Is Poverty? Who Asks? Who Answers?" *Poverty in Focus*, (International Poverty Center: United Nations Development Programme, December 2006) 3-4.

72. ACLU, "Stop Anti-Gay Bullying: Seth's Story," American Civil Liberties Union website, 2011, http://www.aclu.org/lgbt-rights/stop-anti-gay-bullying-seths-story.

73. Rachel Aviv, "Netherland," *The New Yorker*, December 10, 2012, 60-69.

74. Joseph G. Kosciw, Emily A. Greytak, Mark J. Bartkiewicz, Madeln J. Boesen, Neal A. Palmer, The 2011 National School Climate Survey: The Experiences of Lesbian, Gay, Bisexual and Transgender Youth in Our Nation's Schools (New York: GLSEN, 2012).

75. Amira Hasenbush, Andrew Flores, Angeliki Kastanis, Brad Sears and Gary Gates, *The LGBT Divide, A Data Portrait of LGBT People in the Midwestern, Mountain & Southern States*, (Los Angeles: The Williams Institute, 2014), 2.

76. Jamie Grant, Injustice at Every Turn, 72.

77. M.V. Lee Badgett, Laura E. Durson and Alyssa Schneebaum, *New Patterns of Poverty in the Lesbian, Gay, and Bisexual Community* (Los Angeles: The Williams Institute, June 2013), 12.

78. Burwick, Andrew, Gary Gates, Scott Baumgartner, and Daniel Friend, Human Services for Low Income and At-Risk LGBT Populations: An Assessment of the Knowledge Base and Research Needs, OPRE Report Number 2014-79 (Washington, DC: Office of Planning, Research and Evaluation, Administration for Children and Families, U.S. Department of Health and Human Services, 2014), 32.

79. Jennifer Pizer, Brad Sears, Christy Mallory, Nan Hunter, "Evidence of Persistent and Pervasive Workplace Discrimination Against LGBT People: the Need for Federal Legislation Prohibiting Discrimination and Providing for Equal Employment Benefits," *Loyola of Los Angeles Law Review* 45, no. 3 (2012): 723.

80. Ibid., 727.

81. Burwick, Human Services for Low Income and At-Risk LGBT Populations, 22.

82. Badgett, New Patterns of Poverty in the Lesbian, Gay, and Bisexual Community.

83. Burwick, Human Services for Low Income and At-Risk LGBT Populations, 32.

84. Jamie Grant, Injustice at Every Turn, 2-8.

85. Randy Albelda, M.V. Lee Badgett, Gary J. Gates, Alyssa Schneebaum, *Poverty In the Lesbian, Gay Bisexual Community* (Los Angeles: Williams Institute, March 2009), ii.

86. Jamie Grant, *Injustice at Every Turn*, 33, 51, 72, 106.

87. Allison Auldridge and Robert Espinoza, *Health Equity and LGBT Elders of Color, Recommendations for Policy and Practice,* (New York: Services and Advocacy for GLBT Elders, 2013).

88. Karen I. Fredriksen-Goldsen, Hyun-Jun Kim, Charles A. Emlet, Anna Muraco, Elena A. Eroshea, Charles P. Hoy-Ellis, Jayn Goldsen and Heidi Petry, *The Aging and Health Report: Disparities and Resilience Among Lesbians, Gay, Bisexual, and Transgender Older Adults* (Seattle: Institute for Multigenerational Health, 2011).

89. Jennifer Pizer, Brad Sears, Christy Mallory, Nan Hunter, "Evidence of Persistent and Pervasive Workplace Discrimination Against LGBT People: the Need for Federal Legislation Prohibiting Discrimination and Providing for Equal Employment Benefits," *Loyola of Los Angeles Law Review* 45, no. 3 (2012): 769.

90. Burwick, Human Services for Low Income and At-Risk LGBT Populations, 22, 29, 30.

91. Lawrence v. Texas, 539 US 558, 573 (2003) quoting Planned Parenthood of Southeastern PA. v. Casey, 505 US 833, 851 (1992).

92. United Nations Development Programme, *Human Development Report*, 1990 (New York: Oxford University Press, 1990).

93. Since first report was issued in 1999, a variety of dimensions of development have been examined: knowledge (1990, 2009), political freedom (1990, 1991, 1997, 2004, 2009), human rights (1990, 1995, 1997, 1999, 2000), self-respect (1990, 1995, 1997, 1999, 2000), freedom of action and expression (1992), participation (1993, 1994, 2002, 2005), being creative and productive (1995, 1997, 1998, 1999, 2000), empowerment (1998, 2000), a sense of belonging to a community (1998, 1999, 2000), cultural liberty (2004), and others.

94. United Nations Development Programme, "Human Development Index," *Human Development Reports*, United Nations Development Programme, 2013,

http://hdr.undp.org/en/statistics/hdi/.

95. Ibid.

96 United Nations Development Programme, "Gender Inequality Index," *Human Development Reports*, United Nations Development Programme, 2013,

http://hdr.undp.org/en/statistics/gii/.

97. Sabrina Alkire, "Why the Capability Approach," *Journal of Human Development and Capabilities* 6, no.1 (2005): 115-135; Ingrid Robeyns, "The Capability Approach: A Theoretical Survey," *Journal of Human Development and Capabilities* 6, no.1 (2005): 93-115.

98. Ingrid Robeyns, "The Capability Approach," 103-106.

99. Martha A. Nussbaum, *Creating Capabilities: The Human Development Approach* (Cambridge:Belknap Press, 2011), 33.

100. One, Inc. v. Olesen 355 U.S. 371 (January 13, 1958).

101. Lambda Legal, "About Us: History," Lambda Legal Defense and Education Fund, accessed June 30, 2013,

http://www.lambdalegal.org/about-us/history.

102. Tom Waddell, founder of the Gay Games, quoted on the Gay Games website, http://gaygames.org/wp/about-the-fgg/gay-games-milestones/.

103. George Weinberg, interview by Brooke Gladstone, In Defense of "Homophobia"," On the Media, December 7, 2012, http://www.onthemedia.org/2012/dec/07/defense-homophobia/transcript/.

104. Devor, "Witnessing and Mirroring," 45-46.

105. Mark David Agrast, Juan Carlos Botero, Joel Martinez, Alejandro Ponce, Christine S. Prattorld, *Justice Project Rule of Law Index 2012-2013* (Washington D.C.: The World Justice Project, 2013), 7-20.

106. Freedom House, *Freedom in the World 2013*, (Washington, D.C., Freedom House, 2013),

http://www.freedomhouse.org/report/freedom-world/freedom-world-2013.

107. Hillary Rodham Clinton, "Remarks in Recognition of International Human Rights Day," Secretary of State, December 6, 2011,
http://www.state.gov/secretary/rm/2011/12/178368.htm.

108 Philip Alston, et al., "The Yogyakarta Principles on the Application of International Human Rights Law in Relation to Sexual Orientation and Gender Identity," Yogyakarta: Conference of International Human Rights Experts, 2007,
http://www.yogyakartaprinciples.org/principles_en.htm.

109. Paula Ettelbrick and Alia Trabucco Zeran, "The Impact of the Yogyakarta Principles on International Human Rights Law Development," (2010),
http://www.ypinaction.org/files/02/57/Yogyakarta_Principles_Impact_Tracking_Report.pdf.

110. Nabozny v. Podlesny, 92 F.3d 446 (7th Cir. 1996).

111. Kosciw et al., The 2011 National School Climate Survey, 9.

112. Jaime M. Grant et al., *Injustice at Every Turn*, 69.

113. Gary J. Gates, "LGBT Identity: A Demographer's Perspective," *Loy. L.A. L. Rev.* 45 (2012): 693,
http://digitalcommons.lmu.edu/llr/vol45/iss3/2.

114. Associated Press, "Study Sees Gays as 1.7 Percent of Population," *The Washington Times*, April 7, 2011,
http://www.washingtontimes.com/news/2011/apr/7/study-sees-gays-as-17-percent-of-population/.

115. Family Builders, Legal Services for Children, National Center for Lesbian Rights and the Center for the Study of Social Policy, "Guidelines for Managing Information Related to the Sexual Orientation and Gender Identity and Expression of Children in Child Welfare Systems," January, 2013.

116. LGBT Self-ID Community of Practice, "Where are out LGBT employees?," May 8, 2009,
http://outandequal.org/documents/LGBTSelfIdentificationReport.pdf.

117. Gary Gates and Frank Newport, "Special Report: 3.4% of U.S. Adults Identify as LGBT," Gallup, October 18, 2012,
http://www.gallup.com/poll/158066/special-report-adults-identify-lgbt.aspx.

118. The website "LGBTData.com," lists a number of data gathering efforts undertaken by public agencies. http://www.lgbtdata.com/.

119. U.S. Equal Employment Opportunity Commission, "EEO-1 Frequently Asked Questions and Answers," U.S. Equal Employment Opportunity Commission, http://www.eeoc.gov/employers/eeo1survey/faq.cfm.

120. Burwick, Human Services for Low Income and At-Risk LGBT Populations, xv.

121. Franklin Kameny, quoted David W. Dunlap, "Gay Rights Pioneer, Dies at 86," *New York Times*, October 11, 2011, http://www.nytimes.com/2011/10/13/us/franklin-kameny-gay-rights-pioneer-dies-at-86.html?_r=0.

122. Summary of Argument, Brief of Petitioner at 8,9, Lawrence and Garner v. Texas, No. 02-102 (U.S. Supreme Court, Jan 16, 2003).

123. Tom W. Smith, "Public Attitudes toward Homosexuality," (Chicago: NORC/University of Chicago, September, 2011).

124. Janet Jakobson, Ann Pellegrini, *Love the Sin: Sexual Regulation and the Limits of Tolerance,* (Boston: Beacon Press, 2004), 79.

125. Rev. Ed Bacon, Being gay Is a Gift from God, *The Huffington Post*, October 11, 2011, http://www.huffingtonpost.com/rev-ed-bacon/being-gay-is-a-gift-from-god_b_1005935.html

126. David Fleisher, *The Prop 8 Report: What Defeat in California Can Teach Us About Winning Future Ballot Measures on Same-Sex Marriage*, LGBT Mentoring Project, August 3, 2010, Executive Summary, http://prop8report.lgbtmentoring.org/read-the-report/executive-summary.

127. Senator Feinstein: No on Prop 8, You Tube Video, Uploaded on October 28, 2008, 31 Seconds, https://www.youtube.com/watch?v=U7LdC1RxvZg.

128. PR Newswire, "America Ferrera, Tony Plana & Ana Ortiz Speak Out Against Proposition 8," CBS8.com, October 26, 2008. http://www.cbs8.com/story/9240218/america-ferrera-tony-plana-ana-ortiz-speak-out-against-proposition-8.

129. The Thorons – Don't Eliminate Marriage for Anyone, You Tube Video, Uploaded on September 22, 2008, 38 seconds, https://www.youtube.com/watch?v=l6dBUCi32c8.

130. Gay and Lesbian Alliance Against Defamation, GLAAD, Vote No Amendment 2,
http://www.glaad.org/advertising/library/vote-no-amendment-2.

131. Christian Newswire, "New TV Ad to be Aired During DNC Convention by Florida Stealth 'Gay Rights' Group in Florida is Both Factually Wrong and Attempts to Deceive Democrat Voters," August, 25, 2008,
http://www.christiannewswire.com/news/604707618.html.

132. Molly Ball, "The Marriage Plot: Inside This Year's Epic Campaign for Gay Equality," *The Atlantic*, December, 11, 2012, http://www.theatlantic.com/politics/archive/2012/12/the-marriage-plot-inside-this-years-epic-campaign-for-gay-equality/265865/.

133. David Fleisher, The Prop 8 Report: What Defeat in California Can Teach Us About Winning Future Ballot Measures on Same-Sex Marriage, LGBT Mentoring Project, August 3, 2010, 412 http://prop8report.lgbtmentoring.org/read-the-report/appendices-overview/appendix-l-the-larger-dynamics.

134. Nathaniel Frank, "How Gay Marriage Finally Won at the Polls," Slate, Nov. 7, 2012,
http://www.slate.com/articles/news_and_politics/politics/2012/11/gay_marriage_in_maryland_and_maine_the_inside_strategy.html.

135. Roadmap to Victory, Freedom to Marry,
http://www.freedomtomarry.org/pages/roadmap-to-victory.

136 Cite tom smith NORC report and GALLUP, Marriage, Gay and Lesbian Rights, http://www.gallup.com/poll/1651/gay-lesbian-rights.aspx

137. Brian Powell, Matasha York Quadlin, and Oren Pizmony-Levy, "Public Opinion, the Courts, and Same-sex Marriage: Four Lessons Learned," *Social Currents* 2, no. 1 (2015): 3-12.

Bibliography
(excluding legal and statutory authorities)

Agrast, M., J. Botero, J. Martinez, A. Ponce, and C. Pratt. *WJP Rule of Law Index 2012-2013*. Washington, D.C.: The World Justice Project, 2013.

Albelda, Randy, M.V. Lee Badgett, Gary J. Gates, and Alyssa Schneebaum. "Poverty in the Lesbian, Gay Bisexual Community." Los Angeles: The Williams Institute, March 2009, http://williamsinstitute.law.ucla.edu/research/censu s-lgbt-demographics-studies/poverty-in-the-lesbian-gay-and-bisexual-community/.

Alkire, Sabrina. "Why the Capability Approarch." *Journal of Human Development and Capabilities* 6, no. 1 (2005): 115-135.

Alston, Philip et al. "The Yogyakarta Principles on the Application of International Human Rights Law in Relation to Sexual Orientation and Gender Identity." Yogyakarta: Conference of International Human Rights Experts. 2007. http://www.yogyakartaprinciples.org/principles_en. htm.

American Civil Liberties Union. "Stop Anti-Gay Bullying: Seth's Story." American Civil Liberties Union. Accessed June 29, 2013. http://www.aclu.org/lgbt-rights/stop-anti-gay-bullying-seths-story.

American Psychiatric Association. *Diagnostic and Statistical Manual of Mental Disorders.* III-R ed. Washington D.C.: American Psychiatric Association, 1987.

———. *Diagnostic and Statistical Manual of Mental Disorders*, edited by Gruenberg, Ernest M.,. 2nd ed. Vol. 2. Washington D.C.: American Psychiatric Association, 1968.

———. *Diagnostic and Statistical Manual: Mental Disorders.* Vol. 1. Washington, D.C.: American Psychiatric Association Mental Hospital Service, 1952.

———. "Position Statement on Homosexuality and Civil Rights." *American Journal of Psychiatry* 131, no. 4 (1974): 497.

Associated Press. "Study Sees Gays as 1.7 Percent of Population." *The Washington Times,* April 7, 2011. http://www.washingtontimes.com/news/2011/apr/7/study-sees-gays-as-17-percent-of-population/.

Auldridge, Allison and Robert Espinoza. *Health Equity and LGBT Elders of Color, Recommendations for Policy and Practice.* New York: Service and Advocacy for GLBT Elders, 2013.

Aviv, Rachel. Netherland. *The New Yorker*, December 10, 2012, 60-69.

Badgett, Lee M.V., Laura E. Durson, and Alyssa Schneebaum, *New Patterns of Poverty in the Lesbian,*

Gay, and Bisexual Community, Los Angeles: The Williams Institute, June 2013.

Bacon, Rev. Ed. Being Gay Is a Gift from God. The Huffington Post, October 11, 2011. http://www.huffingtonpost.com/rev-ed-bacon/being-gay-is-a-gift-from-god_b_1005935.html

Ball, Molly. The Marriage Plot: Inside This Year's Epic Campaign for Gay Equality. *The Atlantic*, December 11, 2012. http://www.theatlantic.com/politics/archive/2012/12/the-marriage-plot-inside-this-years-epic-campaign-for-gay-equality/265865/.

Beals, K.P., L. A. Peplau, and S. L. Gable. "Stigma Management and Well-Being: The Role of Perceived Social Support, Emotional Processing, and Suppression." *Personality and Social Psychology Bulletin* 35, no. 7 (2009): 867-879.

Berube, Allan. *Coming Out Under Fire*. New York: The Free Press, 1990.

Burwick, Andrew, Gary Gates, Scott Baumgartner, and Daniel Friend, *Human Services for Low Income and At-Risk LGBT Populations: An Assessment of the Knowledge Base and Research Needs, OPRE Report Number 2014-79*. Washington, DC: Office of Planning, Research and Evaluation, Administration for Children and Families, U.S. Department of Health and Human Services, 2014.

Cass, Vivienne C. "Homosexual Identity Formation: Testing a Theoretical Model." *Journal of Sex Research* 20, no. 2 (1984): 143-167.

Chambers, Robert "What Is Poverty? Who Asks? Who Answers?" in *Poverty in Focus*, ed. Dag Ehrenpreis. Brasilia: United Nations Development Programme International Poverty Center, December 2006.

Christian Newswire. "New TV Ad to be Aired During DNC Convention by Florida Stealth 'Gay Rights' Group in Florida is Both Factually Wrong and Attempts to Deceive Democrat Voters." August 25, 2008.
http://www.christiannewswire.com/news/60470761 8.html.

Clinton, Hillary Rodham. "Remarks in Recognition of International Human Rights Day." Secretary of State. December 6, 2011.
www.state.gov/secretary/rm/2011/12/178368.htm.

Coleman, et al. "Standards of Care for the Health of Transsexual, Transgender and Gender Non-Conforming People, Version 7." *International Journal of Transgenderism* 13, no. 4 (2011): 165-232.

Cory, Donald Webster. *The Homosexual in America: A Subjective Approach.* New York: Greenberg, 1956.

Dannemeyer, William. *Shadow in the Land: Homosexuality in America.* San Francisco: Ignatius, 1989.

D'Emilio, John. *Sexual Politics, Sexual Communities: The Making of a Homosexual Minority in the United States, 1940-1970*. Chicago: University of Chicago Press, 1998.

DeNavas-Walt, Carmen, Bernadette D. Proctor, and Jessica C. Smith. *U.S. Census Bureau, Current Population Reports, P60-243, Income, Poverty, and Health Insurance Coverage in the United States: 2011*. Washington, DC: U.S. Government Printing Office, 2012.

Devor, Aaron H. "Witnessing and Mirroring: A Fourteen Stage Model of Transsexual Identity Formation." *Journal of Gay and Lesbian Psychotherapy* 8, (2004): 41-67.

Drescher, Jack and Kenneth J. Zucker, eds. *Ex-Gay Research: Analyzing the Spitzer Study and its Relation to Science, Religion, Politics, and Culture*. New York: Harrington Park Press, 2006.

Drescher, Jack, Peggy Cohen-Kettenis, and Sam Winter. "Minding the Body: Situating Gender Identity Diagnosis in the ICD-11." *International Review of Psychiatry* 26, no. 6 (December 2012): 568-577.

Schrimshaw, E.W., K. Siegel, M. J. Downing Jr, and J. T. Parsons. "Disclosure And Concealment Of Sexual Orientation And The Mental Health Of Non-Gay-Identified, Behaviorally Bisexual Men." *Journal of Consulting and Clinical Psychology* 81, no. 1 (2013): 141- 153.

Ettelbrick, Paula and Alia Trabucco Zeran. *The Impact of the Yogyakarta Principles on International Human Rights Law Development.* Geneva: ARC International, 2010. http://www.ypinaction.org/files/02/57/Yogyakarta _Principles_Impact_Tracking_Report.pdf.

Family Builders, Legal Services for Children, National Center for Lesbian Rights and the Center for the Study of Social Policy. *Guidelines for Managing Information Related to the Sexual Orientation and Gender Identity and Expression of Children in Child Welfare Systems.* Oakland: Family Builders By Adoption, January 2013.

Fleisher, David. *The Prop 8 Report: What Defeat in California Can Teach Us About Winning Future Ballot Measures on Same-Sex Marriage.* Los Angeles: LGBT Mentoring Project, August 3, 2010. http://prop8report.lgbtmentoring.org/read-the-report/appendices-overview/appendix-l-the-larger-dynamics.

Frable, D.E.S., L. Platt, and S. Hoey. "Concealable Stigmas And Positive Self-Perceptions: Feeling Better Around Similar Others." *Journal of Personality and Social Psychology* 74, no. 4 (1998): 909-922.

Frank, Nathaniel "How Gay Marriage Finally Won at the Polls," Slate, Nov. 7, 2012, http://www.slate.com/articles/news_and_politics/politics/2012/11/gay_marriage_in_maryland_and_maine_the_inside_strategy.html.

Fredriksen-Goldsen, K.I., H. J. Kim, and S. E. Barkan. "Disability Among Lesbian, Gay, And Bisexual Adults: Disparities In Prevalence And Risk." *American Journal of Public Health 102*, no. 1 (2011): e16-e21.

Fredriksen-Goldsen, K.I., H.J. Kim, C.A. Emlet, A. Muraco, E.A. Erosheva, C.P Hoy-Ellis, J. Goldsen, and H. Petry. *The Aging and Health Report: Disparities and Resilience among Lesbian, Gay, Bisexual, and Transgender Older Adults.* Seattle: Institute for Multigenerational Health, 2011.

Freedom House. *Freedom in the World 2013.* Washington, DC: Freedom House. 2013. http://www.freedomhouse.org/report/freedom-world/freedom-world-2013.

Frijns, T., and C. Finkenauer. "Longitudinal Associations Between Keeping A Secret And Psychosocial Adjustment In Adolescence." *International Journal of Behavioral Development* 33, no. 2 (2009): 145-154.

Frost, D.M. and I.H. Meyer. "Internalized Homophobia and Relationship Quality Among Lesbians, Gay Men, And Bisexuals." *Journal of Counseling Psychology* 56, vol. 1(2009): 97-109.

Gates, Gary and Frank Newport. "Special Report: 3.4% of U.S. Adults Identify as LGBT." *Gallup.* 2012. http://www.gallup.com/poll/158066/special-report-adults-identify-lgbt.aspx.

Gates, Gary J."LGBT Identity: A Demographer's Perspective," 45 Loyola of Los Angeles Law Review 45, no. 3 (2012): 693-714. http://digitalcommons.lmu.edu/llr/vol45/iss3/2.

———. *LGBT Parenting in the United States.* Los Angeles: The Williams Institute, 2013.

General Accounting Office. *Defense of Marriage Act Update to Prior Report,* GAO-04-353R, Washington, D.C.: General Accounting Office, January 23, 2004. http://www.gao.gov/new.items/d04353r.pdf.

Grant, Jaime M., Lisa A. Mottet, Justin Tanis, Jack Harrison, Jody L. Herman, and Mara Keisling. *Injustice at Every Turn: A Report of the National Transgender Discrimination Survey.* Washington: National Center for Transgender Equality and National Gay and Lesbian Task Force, 2011.

Grocholewski, Cardinal Zenon. "Instruction Concerning the Criteria for the Discernment of Vocations with regard to Persons with Homosexual tendencies in view of their Admission to the Seminary and to Holy Orders." Congregation for Catholic Education. 2005. http://www.vatican.va/roman_curia/congregations/ccatheduc/documents/rc_con_ccatheduc_doc_20051104_istruzione_en.html.

Haeberle, Erwin J. "Chronology of Sex Research: II. Pioneers (1896-1936)." Archive for Sexology. Accessed 2013.
http://www.sexarchive.info/GESUND/ARCHIV/CHR06.HTM.

Hampton, Chris. "Why ENDA Matters: True Stories of Anti-LGBT Employment Discrimination From the ACLU." *ACLU: Blog of Rights*, 2009.

Hasenbush, Amira, Andrew Flores, Angeliki Kastanis, Brad Sears, and Gary Gates. *The LGBT Divide, A Data Portriat of LGBT People in the Midwestern, Mountain and Southern States*. Los Angeles: The Williams Institute, 2014.

Hatzenbuehler, M.L., A. Bellatorre, Y. Lee, B. Finch, P. Muennig, and K. Fiscella. "Structural Stigma and All-Cause Mortality In Sexual Minority Populations." *Social Science and Medicine* 103 (2013): 33-41.

Herdt, G. and A. Boxer. *Children of Horizons*. Boston, MA: Beacon Press, 1996.

Herek, Gregory M. "Beyond 'Homophobia': Thinking about Sexual Prejudice and Stigma in the Twenty-First Century." *Sexuality Research and Social Policy* 1, no. 2 (2004): 6-24.

Human Rights Campaign. "Mission Statement." Human Rights Campaign. 2013. http://www.hrc.org/the-hrc-story/mission-statement.

Institute for Development Studies. *Sexuality and Development, IDS Policy Briefing* 29. Brighton: Institute for Development Studies, April 2006.

Jakobson, Janet and Ann Pellegrini. Love the Sin: Sexual Regulation and the Limits of Tolerance. Boston: Beacon Press, 2004.

Jorgensen, Christine. *Christine Jorgensen: A Personal Autobiography*. San Francisco: Cleis, 2000.

Kameny, Franklin, quoted in David W. Dunlap. "Gay Rights Pioneer, Dies at 86." *New York Times*, October 11, 2011. http://www.nytimes.com/2011/10/13/us/franklin-kameny-gay-rights-pioneer-dies-at-86.html?_r=0.

Kinsey, Alfred C., Wardell B. Pomeroy, and Clyde E. Martin. *Sexual Behavior in the Human Male*. Philadelphia: W.B. Saunders, 1948.

Klawitter, Marieka. "Multilevel Analysis of the Effects of Antidiscrimination Policies on Earnings by Sexual Orientation." *Journal of Policy Analysis and Management* 30, no. 2 (2011): 334-358.

Kosciw, J. G., E. A. Greytak, M. J. Bartkiewicz, and N. A. Palmer. *The 2011 National School Climate Survey: The Experiences of Lesbian, Gay, Bisexual and Transgender Youth in our Nation's Schools*. New York: GLSEN, 2012.

Lambda Legal, "FY 2011-FY2014 Lambda Legal Strategic Plan, Mission Statement," Lambda Legal. 2010. http://www.lambdalegal.org/sites/default/files/pub lications/downloads/fs_fy-2011-14-lambda-legal-strategic-plan_1.pdf.

Lambda Legal. "About Us: History." Lamdba Legal. Accessed June 30, 2013, http://www.lambdalegal.org/about-us/history.

LGBT Self-ID Community of Practice, "Where are out LGBT employees?" May 8, 2009. http://outandequal.org/documents/LGBTSelfIdent ificationReport.pdf

Lick, D.J., L. E. Durso, and K. L. Johnson. "Minority Stress And Physical Health Among Sexual Minorities." *Perspectives On Psychological Science* 8, no. 5 (2013): 521-548.

Lobel, Jules. *Sucess without Victory: Lost Legal Battles and the Long Road to Justice in America.* New York: New York University, 2006.

Marshal, M.P., L. J. Dietz, M. S. Friedman, R. Stall, H. A. Smith, J. McGinley, and D. A. Brent. "Suicidality And Depression Disparities Between Sexual Minority And Heterosexual Youth: A Meta-Analytic Review." *Journal of Adolescent Health* 49, no. 2 (2011): 115-123.

Meyer, Ilan. "Prejudice, Social Stress, And Mental Health In Lesbian, Gay And Bisexual Populations: Conceptual Issues And Research Evidence." *Psychological Bulletin* 129, no. 5 (2003): 674-697.

Movement Advancement Project, Center for American Progress, and Human Rights Campaign. *A Broken Bargain: Discrimination, Fewer Benefits and More Taxes for LGBT Workers.* 2013. http://www.lgbtmap.org/file/a-broken-bargain-full-report.pdf.

Nussbaum, Martha A. *Creating Capabilities: The Human Development Approach.* Cambridge: Belknap, 2011.

Obama, Barack. "Remarks by the President at a Campaign Event, Tampa, FL." The White House Office of the Press Secretary. October 25, 2012. http://www.whitehouse.gov/the-press-office/2012/10/25/remarks-president-campaign-event-tampa-fl.

Pachankis, John. "The Psychological Implications Of Concealing A Stigma: A Cognitive- Affective-Behavioral Model." *Psychological Bulletin* 133, no.2 (2007): 328-345.

Park, Andrew and Tiffany Palmer. *Survey of Statutory Rights Associated with Marriage in Pennsylvania.* Philadelphia: The Center for Lesbian and Gay Civil Rights, March 23, 1999. http://www.pacourts.us/assets/files/setting-3220/file-2931.pdf?cb=3f151f.

Pizer, Jennifer, Brad Sears, Christy Mallory, Nan Hunter. "Evidence of Persistent and Pervasive Workplace Discrimination Against LGBT People: the Need for Federal Legislation Prohibiting Discrimination and Providing for Equal Employment Benefits." *Loyola of Los Angeles Law Review* 44, no. 3 (2012): 715–779.

Powell, Brian, Matasha York Quadlin, and Oren Pizmony-Levy. "Public Opinion, the Courts, and Same-sex Marriage: Four Lessons Learned." *Social Currents* 2, no. 1 (2015): 3-12.

PR Newswire. "America Ferrera, Tony Plana & Ana Ortiz Speak Out Against Proposition 8." CBS8.com, October 26, 2008.
http://www.cbs8.com/story/9240218/america-ferrera-tony-plana-ana-ortiz-speak-out-against-proposition-8.

Ragins, Belle Rose et al. "Making the Invisible Visible: Fear and Disclosure of Sexual Orientation at Work." *J. Applied Psychol.* 92 (2007): 1103-1112.

Ratzinger, Joseph Cardinal. "Letters to the Bishops of the Catholic Church on the Pastoral Care of Homosexual Persons." Congregation for the Doctrine of the Faith. 1986, no. 3.
http://www.vatican.va/roman_curia/congregations/cfaith/documents/rc_con_cfaith_doc_19861001_homosexual-persons_en.html.

Ringo, Peter. "Media Roles in Female-to-Male Transsexual and Transgender Identity Formation." *The International Journal of Transgenderism* 6, no. 3 (2002).

Robeyns, Ingrid. "The Capability Approach: A Theoretical Survey." *Journal of Human Development and Capabilities* 6, no. 1 (2005): 93-117.

Smith, Tom W. *Public Attitudes toward Homosexuality*. Chicago: NORC/University of Chicago, September, 2011.

Subcommittee on Investigations, Committee on Expenditures in the Executive Departments, *Employment of Homosexuals and Other Sex Perverts in Government*, 81st Congress, Doc. No. 241 at 3-5 (December 15, 1950).

Swartz, Aaron. "Why I Am Not Gay." *Raw Thought*. 2001. http://www.aaronsw.com/weblog/notgay.

Tilcsik, Andras. "Pride and Prejudice: Employment Discrimination Against Openly Gay Men in the United States." *American Journal of Sociology* 117, no. 2 (2011): 586-626.

U.S. Equal Employment Opportunity Commission. "EEO-1 Frequently Asked Questions and Answers." http://www.eeoc.gov/employers/eeo1survey/faq.cfm.

United Nations Development Programme. "Gender Inequality Index (GII)." 2013. http://hdr.undp.org/en/statistics/gii/.

————. "Human Development Index." 2013, http://hdr.undp.org/en/statistics/hdi/.

————. . *Human Development Report, 1990*. New York: Oxford University, 1990, and various subsequent annual Human Development Reports.

Vaid, Urvashi. *Virtual Equality: The Mainstreaming of Gay and Lesbian Liberation*. New York: Anchor, 1995.

Waddell, Tom and Dick Schaap. *Gay Olympian*. 1st ed. New York: Alfred A. Knopf, 1996.

Weinberg, George H. *Society and the Healthy Homosexual*. New York: St. Martin's, 1972.

Weinberg, George. "Interview by Brook Gladstone. In Defense of 'Homophobia'." *On the Media*. NPR-WNYC, December 7, 2012. http://www.onthemedia.org/2012/dec/07/defense-homophobia/transcript/.

Wilber, Shannan, Caitlin Ryan, and Jody Marksamer. *CWLA Best Practice Guidlines*. Washington, D.C.: Child Welfare League of America, Inc., 2006.

Yoshino, Kenji. Speak Now: Marriage Equality on Trial. New York: Crown Publishers, 2015.

Yoshino, Kenji. "Covering." *Yale Law Journal* 111, no. 4 (2002):769–939.

Yoshino, Kenji. Covering: The Hidden Assault on our Civil Rights. New York: Random House, 2007.

Acknowledgments

The concepts in this book were initially presented at the opening plenary session of the 2013 meeting of the Funders for Lesbian and Gay Issues. I am grateful to the staff and board of Funders for providing me with an opportunity to refine my ideas and engage in commentary and discussion about the content. My thanks go to Carla Sutherland for feedback when I first began making presentations on the capabilities approach. My sincere gratitude goes to Urvashi Vaid for her encouragement and inspiration. I am also grateful for the thorough feedback of John Taylor and my colleagues at Wellspring Advisors, LLC. Adam Whitehurst, Alexis Swanson and Taylor Brown provided invaluable editorial assistance. Claibourn Hamilton provided much appreciated input on early concepts for cover design. I would also like to thank my colleagues at the Williams Institute, UCLA School of Law, for their assistance and inspiration, particularly Adam Romero for reviewing an early draft.

About the Author

Mr. Park is currently Director of International Programs at the Williams Institute, University of California Los Angeles School of Law. Prior to that he was a Program Director at Wellspring Advisors, LLC, in New York, where he has directed a variety of human rights programs. He served as the coordinator of the International Human Rights Funders Group and co-chair of the Global Philanthropy Project. After law school at George Washington University in Washington, DC, he worked at the U.S. Equal Employment Opportunity Commission as a trial attorney and subsequently in the Philadelphia District Office as an Administrative Judge. In Philadelphia, he founded the Center for Lesbian and Gay Civil Rights and served as its executive director for five years, where he successfully led a coalition to defeat an anti-gay ballot initiative and pass domestic partnership legislation. Park has taught at the University of Pennsylvania Law School and the George Washington School of Law. He was co-chair of the Gay and Lesbian Attorneys of Washington, DC (GAYLAW), and has been an officer of the Gay and Lesbian Lawyer of Philadelphia (GALLOP), the National Council of EEOC Locals, AFGE, AFL-CIO, the Liberty City Democratic Club.

www.ingramcontent.com/pod-product-compliance
Lightning Source LLC
Chambersburg PA
CBHW050114280326
41933CB00010B/1097